Spiritual Gifts

HOLY SPIRIT
ESSENTIALS

Spiritual Gifts

LEARN TO DEFINE AND UTILIZE YOUR GOD-GIVEN GIFTS

SAM STORMS

Chosen
a division of Baker Publishing Group
Minneapolis, Minnesota

Originally published by Servant Publications in 2002.
Second edition published by Regal in 2012.

Published by Chosen Books
Minneapolis, Minnesota
ChosenBooks.com

Chosen Books is a division of
Baker Publishing Group, Grand Rapids, Michigan

Library of Congress Cataloging-in-Publication Data
Names: Storms, C. Samuel, author
Title: Spiritual gifts : learn to define and utilize your God-given gifts / Sam Storms.
Other titles: Beginner's guide to spiritual gifts
Description: Minneapolis, Minnesota : Chosen, a division of Baker Publishing Group, [2025] | Series: Holy Spirit essentials | "Originally published by Servant Publications in 2002"—Title page verso.
Identifiers: LCCN 2025009394 | ISBN 9780800778361 paperback | ISBN 9780800778378 casebound | ISBN 9781493452323 ebook
Subjects: LCSH: Gifts, Spiritual
Classification: LCC BT767.3 .S76 2025 | DDC 234/.13—dc23/eng/20250710
LC record available at https://lccn.loc.gov/2025009394

Cover design by Chris Gilbert, Studio Gearbox

Although the men and women whose stories are told in this book are real, many of their names have been changed to protect their privacy.

25 26 27 28 29 30 31   7 6 5 4 3 2 1

CONTENTS

ONE

Power Outage!

Some things I see in the Church today encourage me. Movements rise, books are sold, conferences abound—but when I look beyond the flurries of Christian activity, I see a large gap between what Christians say they *know* and the way they *live*.

Lives get broken, bodies and marriages suffer, and people just give up and walk away. Self and sin flourish—while the poor and the hungry stay that way.

So, what's wrong? I'm convinced that the problem is power—or really, a *lack of power*. The Church at large is suffering from a power outage!

Where I'm Coming From

Let me tell you where I've been. Born and raised a Southern Baptist, I attended the same church until I went to seminary. I've pastored a Presbyterian church, and attended independent Bible churches, a Vineyard congregation, and a charismatic Anglican fellowship. I've pastored Bridgeway Church and taught theology at a Christian college. Through these experiences, my conviction about what's wrong with the Church has solidified.

Here's what I see: The Church needs a fresh infusion of *power*—I mean spiritual power. We desperately need the power of Jesus through the activity of the Holy Spirit!

When I read the book of Acts, I see power operating in the lives of those believers—Holy Spirit power that prompted life-changing actions and concrete impact.

It's available to us, too. How? *Spiritual gifts!* God gives these gifts through the Holy Spirit to lead His Church into the fullness of His plans.

"Correct" doctrine won't help us. The Church needs to walk in truth, set aflame by the power of the Holy Spirit to bring what we *know* to bear on how we *live*—how we pray, how we love, and how we witness.

Let me tell you what I've found. For the first fifteen years of my ministry, I was a "cessationist." This means I believed that the so-called "miraculous gifts of the Holy Spirit" *ceased* in the first century. The gifts of prophecy, speaking in tongues, healing, miracles, words of wisdom, words of knowledge, and the discerning of spirits were finished, done away with. It's the view of many evangelicals.

I later realized that the Bible doesn't teach this.

But the hardest change wasn't my theology; it was my prejudices. Most people who claimed to exercise spiritual gifts embarrassed me. I was offended by their unpolished ways and their exuberant displays. I was afraid of emotionalism, of losing control—and (mostly) of being rejected by my peers. Even deeper was the fear of what might happen if I were to lay down control of my life, mind, and emotions to the Holy Spirit. It might end up costing me my hard-earned *status* in the evangelical community.

This fear kept me distanced from anything that linked me with "charismatic" people. My pride and fear influenced me more than Scripture did. Fear of being associated with the "un-learned" powerfully affected the way I read Scripture.

By the way, if all of this sounds like arrogance, self-righteousness, and "being right" above everything else, that's precisely what it was. Pride is the mother of all sins, and I had a mother of a pride problem.

Again, most cessationists believe that once the apostles died, the operation of some gifts (especially prophecy, tongues, interpretation of tongues, and miracles) ceased. Most would say that miracles *can* happen—but don't expect them! And the expression of *any* of those gifts named above is forbidden in many churches.

Yet if we reject spiritual gifts, we turn from God's empowering —and in a sense, we turn from God. Most cessationists probably don't *mean* to resist God, but when we deny His gifts, we deny *Him*. Cessationist theology changes how we encounter the enemy and minister to the broken. But why wouldn't we build God's Kingdom with the tools *God has provided*? As I said, we've tried our own good ideas (human effort, "the flesh")— and how well is *that* working?

Although most cessationists believe God can and occasionally does heal people today, they often say a person who has "the gift of healing" or "the gift of miracles" must exercise supernatural power at *their* will, not God's will—on any occasion, at any time, with the same degree of success as the apostles. This fallacy ignores God as Giver. But then again, seeing how *few* miracles there are in most churches, it's easy for cessationists to conclude that such gifts no longer operate in the Church.

God in His Gifts

Here's a basic but crucial principle: Spiritual gifts are *God Himself* in us, energizing our souls, imparting revelation to our minds, infusing power into our wills, and working His sovereign and gracious purposes through us. Spiritual gifts are God present in, with, and through human thoughts, deeds, words, and love.

The language Paul uses to make this point is clear. Since we'll talk mainly about the gifts listed in 1 Corinthians 12:4–11, let's notice what Paul says there about the source and energy of the gifts:

> Now there are varieties of gifts, but the same Spirit. And there are varieties of ministries, and the same Lord. There are varieties of effects, but the same God who works all things in all persons. But to each one is given the manifestation of the Spirit for the common good. For to one is given the word of wisdom through the Spirit, and to another the word of knowledge according to the same Spirit; to another faith by the same Spirit, and to another gifts of healing by the one Spirit, and to another the effecting of miracles, and to another prophecy, and to another the distinguishing of spirits, to another various kinds of tongues, and to another the interpretation of tongues. But one and the same Spirit works all these things, distributing to each one individually just as He wills.

Look at the word translated "manifestation" (*phanerosis*) in verse 7. Paul is saying that the Spirit is shown forth, made evident, whenever spiritual gifts are used. The gifts display God's action through the Spirit, resulting in clear expressions of His power. Gifts are "God going public."

Spiritual gifts are not the only way God shows His power —He can show His power in any way He chooses! The Spirit brings joy, peace, and hope (see Romans 15:13) just as much as He brings "signs and wonders" (Romans 15:19). But clearly, the gifts described in the New Testament are a main way through which God's power comes to our otherwise listless lives.

What I have in mind is the operation of those gifts listed in 1 Corinthians 12:7–10, all of which, I believe, are available to the Church today.

Why the "Nine"?

Why focus only on the gifts listed in 1 Corinthians 12:7–10, when there are also other gifts important to the Church?

1. These nine gifts (word of wisdom, word of knowledge, faith, healing, miracles, prophecy, distinguishing of spirits, tongues, interpretation of tongues) are less well understood than other gifts like mercy or teaching (see Romans 12:7–8).
2. These nine gifts have sparked many divisive debates. I aim to eliminate prejudices not only about these gifts, but also about the people who use them.
3. The Church desperately needs God's supernatural power. Although "the same God" energizes all spiritual gifts (1 Corinthians 12:6), these nine gifts are more visible and impactful. The Church needs the life-changing, Christ-honoring power of Holy Spirit activity. The Church needs to know that such gifts are available and understand how they function.

I've written this book to *educate* you—so that, free of fear and misunderstanding, you can receive God's spiritual gifts for you.

I also want you to be equipped to *use* the gifts God gives you. We need to learn *how* and *when* and *for whom* these gifts are designed, so that when we use His gifts, God is glorified and we are edified.

Finally, I want you to be *expectant* about what God can do. I want your confidence in both God's goodness and His greatness to intensify. Expectant folks are ready to receive God's gifts!

That's why I've written this book. That's why I hope you'll read it.

TWO

Defining Our Terms

We call them "spiritual gifts." What does the Bible call them? Let's look at the four Greek words in the New Testament that commonly refer to spiritual gifts: *charisma*, *pneumatikon*, *diakonia*, and *energema*. Defining our terms will help us gain a fuller understanding of spiritual gifts and avoid common misconceptions about them.

Charisma

The most familiar term Paul used for the gifts of God is the Greek word *charisma*. *Charisma* is a gift, something God's grace has given. For example, eternal life is a *charisma* (see Romans 6:23).

Pneumatikon

In 1 Corinthians 12:1, Paul used the word *pneumatikon* ("spirituals," i.e., spiritual things), but he shifted to the use of *charisma* in verse 4 and following. This is because Paul emphasizes that such gifts come through God's gracious enabling. So, *all* gifts are charismatic, not just healings and miracles. Helping and serving and giving are charismatic, too. In that sense, all Christians are "charismatics."

Diakonia

Charisma points us to the origin of spiritual gifts. *Diakonia* (often translated "ministries" or "services") points to their purpose. *All spiritual gifts are designed to serve and help others.* They are never given for personal advancement, status, power, or popularity. In 1 Peter 4:10–11, the verb form of *diakonia* is used twice of gifted believers "serving" one another. Spiritual gifts are *gifts with responsibilities*, not status symbols.

Energema

Spiritual gifts are also described by the term *energema*, translated "effects" (NASB) or "working" (NIV). Here, Paul emphasizes that gifts are the effect or fruit of God's power. All spiritual gifts are *energized* by the power of the Holy Spirit in and through the believer. In 1 Corinthians 12:6, Paul wrote, "There are varieties of effects [*energematon*], but the same God who works [*ho energon*] all things in all persons." So, *gifts are the operations of God's energy through individual believers.*

God-Given Grace-Gifts

Notice how Paul repeats that *one* Spirit is the source of a *variety* of gifts. Gifts come "through the Spirit . . . according to the same Spirit . . . by the same Spirit . . . by the one Spirit" (1 Corinthians 12:8–9). Indeed, it is "one and the same Spirit" (verse 11) who gives gifts according to His will.

If the Holy Spirit is sovereign in giving gifts, He is also sovereign in withholding them. It all depends on what God desires for that moment in His Church. Rather than "claim" a gift, we submit to His sovereign will regarding it (compare verses 9 and 11).

When we put these four Greek words together, we discover that all spiritual gifts (*charismata*) are acts of service or ministry (*diakonia*), which are produced (*energema*) through us by the triune God—*pneuma* (the Holy Spirit) in verse 4, *kurios* (the Lord Jesus) in verse 5, and *theos* (God the Father) in verse 6.

In light of this, let's define a spiritual gift as "a God-given grace-gift to the Body of Christ, spiritually energizing His people to serve the Body and communicate Jesus' wisdom, power, and love."

Got it? Good! Let's go!

Myths and Misconceptions

Here are a few common myths about spiritual gifts I want to look at with you:

Myth #1: Only pastors or super-saints get miraculous spiritual gifts.

No! The apostle Paul says that to "each one," male and female, young and old, has been given the manifestation of the Spirit (1 Corinthians 12:7). According to Romans 12:3 and 6, if you have grace, you have a gift (see also Ephesians 4:7; 1 Peter 4:10).

On the Day of Pentecost, Peter quoted Joel's prophecy from Joel chapter 2 to prove that gifts such as prophecy and tongues would be given to "all mankind," including "your sons and your daughters," "young men," "old men," as well as "male and female servants" (Acts 2:17–18). They are for every believer!

Others besides the apostles exercised miraculous gifts. The seventy sent by Jesus cast out demons (see Luke 10:9, 19–20). The 120 gathered at Pentecost spoke in tongues. Philip performed miracles and was miraculously transported (see Acts 8). Ananias, a believer in Damascus, prayed for Saul's eyes to be opened (see Acts 9). Four young single women at Caesarea were prophets (see Acts 21:8–9). Believers in Galatia performed miracles (see Galatians 3:5). And there are many more examples in Scripture!

In 1 Corinthians 12:7–10, Paul mentions how God's Spirit gives prophecy, faith, miracles, etc. to God's people so they can build each other up. Homemakers and farmers, along with apostles and deacons, receive the gifts of the Spirit "for the common good" of the Church (verse 7).

Myth #2: When you believed, you got all the gifts you will ever get.

Wait! How many physical gifts have you received since you were born? Why didn't they all come at once? Because over time you grew, you changed, you needed something you didn't yet have. So, as it is in the natural, it also is in the spiritual.

Paul wrote, "Pursue love, yet desire earnestly spiritual gifts, but especially that you may prophesy" (1 Corinthians 14:1). He commanded us to earnestly desire a new spiritual gift (see verses 12, 39.) In 1 Corinthians 12:31, Paul wrote, "Earnestly desire the *greater* gifts" (emphasis added). In 1 Corinthians 14:13, Paul commanded that the person who speaks in tongues "pray that he may interpret." This is addressed to a believer who may have the gift of tongues, but not the gift of interpretation; Paul commanded such an individual to "pray" for it. Clearly, these spiritual gifts can be given after conversion. And if one, why not all?

Myth #3: Miraculous gifts were given to authenticate New Testament apostles.

Wrong! The primary purpose of spiritual gifts is to edify (build up) others. Gifts are "others-oriented." Again, the gifts of 1 Corinthians 12:7–10 are distributed to average Christians "for the common good" (verse 7)—for the benefit of everyone in the Church.

A primary purpose of miraculous gifts is to build up the Body of Christ. Paul pointed out in 1 Corinthians 14:3 that prophecy edifies, exhorts, and consoles others. In verse 4, he said that the one who prophesies "edifies the church." It's the same in verse 5, where he said that tongues, when interpreted, are "so that the church may receive edification." In verse 26, Paul exhorted those in an assembly to be prepared to minister with a psalm, a teaching, a revelation, a tongue, or an interpretation—all of which are designed, he said, for "edification."

My point is this: All the gifts of the Spirit—whether tongues or teaching, prophecy or mercy—were given to edify, build up, encourage, and teach God's people. Clearly, such gifts would continue to function in the Church for the reasons I listed.

Myth #4: Seeking spiritual gifts must mean you don't believe in God's sovereignty.

No! Paul said that the Holy Spirit decides who will get what gift (see 1 Corinthians 12:11, 18). But if God bestows gifts according to His will, how can we pray for gifts according to *our* will? It *could* be that our desire comes from God stirring us up by His Spirit to ask Him for what He wants to give.

While we're on this point, let's consider the ways in which the Spirit may impart His gifts to us. Paul referred to the Spirit sovereignly "distributing" gifts to people, without saying how (1 Corinthians 12:11). For instance, Timothy's gift came to him "through words of prophecy," accompanied by the laying on of hands (literally, "with" the laying on of hands; 1 Timothy 4:14; see also 1 Timothy 1:18; 2 Timothy 1:6). It may be through a prophetic word, or through the laying on of hands, but it is all the sovereign work of the Holy Spirit.

Myth #5: Some people abuse spiritual gifts, so we should avoid spiritual gifts altogether.

Consider: The church at Corinth was awash in spiritual gifts (see 1 Corinthians 1:5–7). But Paul wrote "earnestly *desire spiritual gifts*" to this church where spiritual gifts had been abused

(1 Corinthians 14:1, emphasis added). We might expect Paul to tell them to slow down or stop using these gifts. Instead, Paul commanded them to earnestly seek for more (see 1 Corinthians 12:31; 14:1, 39). The point is this: The solution to the abuse of spiritual gifts is not to stop using them, but to *receive correction*. Paul simply told the Corinthians, "Don't do it less; just do it better!"

To the people in Corinth who were guilty of elitism and fanaticism, Paul said, in effect, "Be eager and zealous for more gifts than you already have." The problem was not spiritual gifts; the problem was immature and unspiritual people.

We must remember that the existence of a fake usually proves that the real exists. It's easy to formulate a theological belief based on looking at what *we may have seen* in others who have faked or abused a gift of God, instead of the beauty of what the Bible describes.

Remember, never develop an unreasonable expectation of *anyone*. No matter how marvelous the manifestation of the Spirit, we humans are "earthen vessels" (2 Corinthians 4:7). We tend to crack! All glory goes to God, not to those who use a gift they have received.

Myth #6: If you have ever used a spiritual gift, you can always use it.

Wrong! Some believe that if you have prophesied once, you can prophesy at will. Or if you have ever prayed and someone was healed, you can heal at will. But these gifts are not *magical powers*. They're *gifts given for a purpose*.

In 1 Corinthians 14:28, Paul expected people to know if someone with the gift of interpretation was present in a meeting. Paul exhorted Timothy not to neglect "the spiritual gift within you" (1 Timothy 4:14). Paul gave titles that describe a continuing function, such as "teachers," "evangelists," or "prophets" (Ephesians 4:11).

In addition, Paul consistently used the *present tense* when he discussed gifts (see 1 Corinthians 12:11), suggesting that gifts are bestowed to meet the need of the moment. Prophecy is dependent on a spontaneous revelation (see 1 Corinthians 14:30); it cannot be exercised at will. Healing is always subject to the sovereign will, purpose, and timing of the Spirit. *The spiritual gifts cannot be worked up or earned; they are gifts, not rewards, nor some "performance" to be given for the approval of others.*

Myth #7: Spiritual gifts aren't necessary, because now we have the Bible, which replaced miracles.

First, the Bible makes no such claim! Consider this: If the Son of God used miracles when He was on earth, how much more would we need them now?

The written Word of God is powerful, but is the Bible capable of doing what Jesus did on earth? "The blind receive sight, the lame walk . . . the dead are raised" (Matthew 11:5 NIV). He relied on the Holy Spirit, using miraculous phenomena to prove that the Kingdom had come upon the people. He told His disciples that they would do "greater works" (John 14:12) because He was going to send His Spirit. He never said that would be true only until we had the Bible!

Myth #8: Spiritual gifts always operate with the same intensity and accuracy.

Not so! Spiritual gifts often vary in intensity, strength, and accuracy (see 1 Corinthians 14:18; 2 Timothy 1:6). Remember, God is the one making this determination. For instance, prophets are to speak in proportion to the confidence they have that what is said is truly of God. They are not to speak beyond what God has revealed. They must be careful never to speak from their own ideas.

Some teachers are more effective than others; some evangelists see more souls come to Christ. Some believers pray more fervently in tongues than others do—apparently as Paul

19

did—and some will have greater capacity for faith. The efficacy of spiritual gifts depends on many factors.

What Paul wrote in 2 Timothy 1:6 indicates that one's gift does not always operate at the same level of intensity, because Timothy is exhorted to "kindle afresh" a spiritual gift.

Myth #9: Those with more spectacular gifts are more spiritual.

This is a myth that few people will *admit to believing*, but that many believe. Those with gifts such as mercy or helps can feel inferior to those with prophecy or tongues. Worse still, those with these more spectacular gifts often *make* other people feel inferior. People whose gifts may draw attention and applause can easily be tricked into thinking more highly of themselves than they should.

In the church at Corinth, the tendency to esteem people more whose gifts had a more visible display became a problem. We may *mistakenly* think that the person with a dynamic gift is more mature or favored of God. Or we think such a person has more of the Holy Spirit. But a person with showy gifts may be less mature than a person with one quiet gift.

Paul's response to this myth is his question to the Corinthians: "What do you have that you did not *receive*? And if you did receive it, why do you boast as if you had not received it?" (1 Corinthians 4:7, emphasis added). We would all do well to heed Paul's question!

Myth #10: The only spiritual gifts God will ever give are those explicitly mentioned in the Bible.

Well, maybe that's wrong. On this point, I have to be careful. But why conclude that God can give only those gifts listed in the New Testament? In Romans 12:6–8, Paul mentioned prophecy, service, teaching, exhortation, giving, leading, and showing mercy. In 1 Corinthians 12:8–10, we read of the word of wisdom, word of knowledge, faith, gifts of healings, the effecting of miracles, prophecy, distinguishing of spirits, tongues, and interpretation of tongues. In the same chapter, Paul mentioned apostles, prophecy, teaching, miracles, gifts of healings, helps, administration, and tongues (see verse 28). Ephesians 4:11 lists apostles, prophets, evangelists, pastors, and teachers as gifts to the Church.

These lists contain an amazing mixture of *what we might regard* as supernatural and natural gifts. Some gifts seem bigger shows of divine power than others. But *Paul made no such distinction*. It is the same God who works all things in all people.

But might there not be new situations, new needs, differing circumstances in differing times and places that call for a manifestation of the Spirit beyond those manifestations Paul described in his own day? I can't prove it, and that's why I'm hesitant to put this myth in the same category as the others. But I see no reason to insist that the lists noted above are *all the gifts that God will ever give*. There's simply no way to know for sure. One thing is certain, however: If there are other gifts that God gives, they will conform to the same principles and rules of practice the Bible sets forth by which all gifts are judged.

THREE

Words of Wisdom and Knowledge

A strange car pulled up outside our church. A distraught father escorted his twenty-year-old son into my office. The son appeared to be struggling with numerous psychological problems, or perhaps demonic oppression. This young man was unable to perform the routine tasks of daily life and was desperate to know what the source of his problem might be.

As we were praying, the name "Megan" popped into my head. (I've altered the names and details of this story.) The impression on my heart was that Megan was the cause of his problem. Through his involvement with her, she had exposed him to demonic influence.

As the young man began to tell me his story, he referred to his girlfriend several times (but not by name), and it was obvious that she played a crucial role in his life. Finally, I asked him what her name was. "Megan," he said.

As it turned out, Megan, who was heavily involved in the occult, had seduced him into an immoral relationship. Understanding this, I knew the Lord was directing me, and I prayed with greater discernment.

About thirty minutes later, another name sprang into my mind: "Derek," with the same clarity as "Megan." But this time, I felt as if Derek were part of the solution. I didn't hesitate on this one. "Does the name Derek mean anything special to you?" I asked.

The young man's face lit up. "Oh, yes! He's my dearest friend —a man older than myself who has been praying for me through this entire mess. In fact, we were on our way to his house to get his advice when we stopped off to talk with you."

God sent me these names to help this young man deal with his problems. Was it a word of knowledge (see 1 Corinthians 12:8), or prophecy? Twice, Paul simply referred to a "revelation" coming to a believer (see 1 Corinthians 14:6, 26), yet he also gave an instance of the "revelation" coming in conjunction with prophecy (see verse 30). Could it be that there are more kinds of what we might call "revelatory" gifts than we realize?

Biblical Precedents

The only place the revelatory gifts are mentioned in the New Testament is in 1 Corinthians 12:8, where Paul provided us with neither a definition nor information about how these gifts are to function in the Body of Christ. But here are some biblical examples of the expressions of these gifts:

> Acts 5:1–11: The Holy Spirit revealed to Peter the secret and sinful activity of Ananias and Sapphira, and spoke a judgment accordingly.

> Acts 8:26–40: The Spirit gave Philip instructions concerning the Ethiopian. Perhaps a word of knowledge?

Acts 9:10–19: Ananias was given "knowledge" of a man named Saul and what to do for him.

Acts 10: Cornelius and Peter both received visions and words of knowledge.

Acts 13:1–3: A word came to the church at Antioch concerning the mission of Paul and Barnabas. Was it a word of wisdom?

Are these revelations? The gift of prophecy? The word of wisdom or word of knowledge? Does it matter? It's still God's sovereign revelation for His purposes.

Perhaps our interpretation of the gift of a "word of wisdom" should reflect Paul's emphasis on the "message" (*word*) of "wisdom" in 1 Corinthians 3, putting the focus less on a revelation about a person and more on the purpose of God in redemptive history. The "word" revealed would explain or unfold God's "wisdom" in bringing salvation to a lost world through the life, death, and resurrection of Jesus. Or again, a word of wisdom may be the ability to articulate life-changing insights into God's purposes for humankind, as well as giving a personal message.

The same may be noted of the word *knowledge*. In 1 Corinthians 8:1–4, 7, 10, *knowledge* appears four times (see also 1 Corinthians 13:2, 8). The "word of knowledge" might therefore be the Spirit-empowered ability to communicate insight into the unfathomable depths of God's gracious work in Christ.

Is a "word of wisdom" or a "word of knowledge" insight that comes spontaneously from the Holy Spirit, or is it a conclusion to which any Christian might come through study of the Scriptures? Some verses seem to support the supernatural, spontaneous, and revelatory nature of this gift. In 1 Corinthians 13:2, Paul mentioned having all knowledge in the same breath with prophecy and faith, both overtly supernatural gifts. Again, in verses 8–12 knowledge is linked with tongues and prophecy to make the point regarding the continuation of the gifts until the Second Coming of Christ. Although no reference is made to the word of knowledge, it seems likely that Paul's use of "knowledge" points back to 1 Corinthians 12:8. We especially note 1 Corinthians 14:6, where knowledge is sandwiched between revelation and prophecy. My sense is that this knowledge is the fruit of a revelatory event that 12:8 indicates is to be spoken ("word" or "message" of knowledge) for the edification of the Church.

Examples of Various Words

In the light of what we've seen about these gifts, how would you classify the following three examples involving Charles Spurgeon, a young lady I know of, and my friend Nancy?

A Gifted Baptist

Charles Spurgeon was perhaps the greatest preacher of the nineteenth century. While preaching at Exeter Hall in London, he once broke off his sermon and pointed in a certain direction, declaring, "Young man, those gloves you are wearing have not been paid for: you have stolen them from your employer."[1]

After the service, a pale and agitated young man approached Spurgeon, begging to speak privately. He laid the pair of gloves on the table and said, "It's the first time I have robbed my master, and I will never do it again. You won't expose me, sir, will you? It would kill my mother if she heard that I had become a thief."[2]

Spurgeon could not have learned this information about the young man from reading the Bible. His insight was undeniably spontaneous, overtly supernatural, and revelatory. (For more great stories, read Spurgeon's autobiography.)

"Walks with a Cough"

It's not unusual for a gift of healing to be imparted in conjunction with a revelatory gift, whether a word of knowledge or prophecy. A young lady attending a church conference was frustrated that her asthma was so severe that she could not sing during worship without using an inhaler.

On the Friday of the conference, she cried out to God for healing, but did not describe her condition to anyone there. She'd had asthma since the age of twelve, but at seventeen the condition worsened. She then began to experience chronic bronchitis (suffering eight to nine months each year) and repeated bouts of pneumonia. She coughed almost constantly, eventually requiring the regular use of steroids and antibiotics. It was so bad that she couldn't climb a flight of stairs without using the inhaler. Taking his cue from the movie *Dances with Wolves*, her husband nicknamed her "Walks with a Cough." She gave birth to a son who also suffered from asthma and was being treated with heavy doses of steroids and breathing treatments, as well as antibiotics.

At the close of the conference on Sunday morning, two days after her prayer of desperation, a man came to the microphone and spoke this word: "There is a lady here today whose name I don't know, but the Lord has told me she has dark hair [which she does]. He also indicated that when you were seventeen years old, you became quite ill, which aggravated your chronic respiratory problems. I would like to pray for you. It may be that the Lord will heal you today."

After hesitating, this lady went forward and identified herself to the man. She also requested prayer for her then four-year-old son. She was instantly healed as the man and his wife prayed for her. In the years since that day, she has had no asthma or pneumonia. Her son also has not needed the steroids or breathing treatments that once were part of his daily life. This is a gift that builds up the Church!

An Amazing Life

My friend Nancy has endured incredible suffering, yet remains strong in the Lord. But even the strong need encouragement. At a conference, I sat beside her as she received a prophetic word that was deeply encouraging. Although the speaker had never met Nancy, he asked her to stand, and he said, "Nancy, I saw the March winds blowing. March is a special month for you. The Lord is going to bless you and give you the spirit of Nathan."

This shows us how a revelation might come accurately to someone who speaks it obediently, although uncertain of its interpretation. When this speaker sensed the Spirit speaking the name "Nathan," he thought of the Old Testament prophet who confronted David. He didn't know (until he was told later) that Nathan is the name of Nancy's son who was killed in a car accident.

The next day, this man again called out Nancy. He told her, "I saw that precious young man who was taken from you. The Lord said, 'I gave him to her in the springtime of the year. And I took him in the middle of the year.' I got a glimpse of him [Nathan] standing before the Lord, and he looks like he's thirty-three years old. That's all he's ever going to look from now on." He was careful to add, "That's not a doctrine, but that's how old he looks."

March is indeed special to Nancy. Her birthday is March 10. Her husband passed away on March 4. The Lord had revealed that Nathan had been "given" to Nancy in the "spring" of the year. Nathan's birthday is April 21. "I took him in the middle of the year," said the Lord. Nathan died on June 4, three months after Nancy's husband.

Nancy had often wondered if Nathan truly knew Jesus before his death. This word encouraged her that he did. As a way of confirming it, the Lord had indicated that Nathan looked "33 years old" on the day when this word was spoken to her. Had Nathan lived, he would have been exactly 33!

Whether it was a word of wisdom, a word of knowledge, or a prophecy, it may be that we don't need to know. What's important for us to know is that God still speaks to benefit, bless, and encourage His children. Let our prayer be, *O Lord, speak! For thy servant heareth!*

FOUR

Faith and Healing

T here is no such thing as the gift of healing. There never
has been. Don't panic! Let me explain—you won't be
disappointed!

Prophetic Providence

My expectations concerning divine healing were radically im-
pacted by what I call an act of prophetic providence. Pastor-
ing in Ardmore, Oklahoma, I was busily preparing my Sunday
sermon. I was still skeptical about the gift of healing, yet I was
preaching through the book of Acts and had come to chapter 3,
in which a man born paralyzed was healed through Peter and
John. My sermon preparation wasn't going well. I was writing words I would soon speak, words that denied—or at least
cast doubt—on the possibility that God might heal someone
like that today.

Then came a knock at the door. My secretary entered with
the day's mail, which didn't usually arrive until well after 1:00
p.m. Here it was, just after 11:00 a.m. For some reason, I put

my pen down and opened the only letter that had arrived. It was from an elderly lady in Wales. I didn't know anyone in Wales. But somehow, this lady had read a book I had written against healing. (That book is now out of print, thankfully.)

Her letter was to the point. She kindly affirmed some of what she had read in my book, but humbly suggested that God would respond with power to our prayers for healing. After reading the letter, I saw what she had added to the envelope. It was the written testimony of a lady named Margery Steven. In 1955, she was afflicted with a severe case of multiple sclerosis, having to be lifted in and out of a wheelchair, her legs and left arm completely useless, her left eye closed, and vision in her right eye virtually gone. She often lost consciousness for hours.

Five years into her illness, Margery had a powerful dream. She saw herself sitting in a chair beside her bed, completely healed. When she awakened, she heard a voice filling the room, a voice she believed to be that of Jesus. He said, "Tarry a little longer." But she seemed only to get worse from that day on. Eventually, her speech became so impaired that no one could understand a word she said. Read in her own words what happened next:

> On Monday, July 4, exactly five months after God had spoken to me, my Lord healed me, in the very chair of which I had dreamed! I had said goodbye to my husband at five minutes to 6:00 on that Monday morning—a helpless woman. At 6:15, my mother gave me a cup of tea. At 6:20, my father and mother lifted me from my bed, strapped me in the chair beside the bed, put a bell in my good hand, to summon aid if needed, and left me alone. Mother went to get my washing water, and my father had gone to get a towel from upstairs. Then, in a matter of seconds, when I was all on my own, my Lord Jesus healed me! I felt a warm glow go over my body. My left foot, which was doubled up, straightened out; my right foot, the toes of which were pointed toward my heel, came back into position. I grasped

the handle of my bedroom door, undid the straps which were about my body, and said, "By faith I will stand," which I did.

With that, I thought of my mother and the shock it would be to her if she came back to find her daughter standing after so many years, so I sat down and called for her. With that, both my parents came running to my room, thinking I was in need of them. I said, "Mum, dear, take my hands. Please don't be afraid; something wonderful has happened." I put out my right arm, and as I did so my left arm came out from behind me and joined the other! It was so wonderful to find I could wear my own wedding ring, which I had not been able to do for years, as my fingers had gotten so thin.

My mother said, "Darling, how wonderful, your hand is warm, and is well again." I said, "Mum, dear, it's more wonderful than that. I can stand." With that, holding her hands, I stood once more on my two feet. Then, gently putting my parents to one side, I said, "Dears, I do not need your help anymore. I'm walking with God." Unaided, I then walked from my bedroom, through the small dining room to the kitchen, my parents following mutely behind me. When I reached the kitchen, I turned and went back into the dining room, and taking off my glasses, I said, "Mum, I can trust God for my hands and feet. I can trust Him for my sight." With that, in a moment, my left eye opened and my sight was fully restored! In fact, Jesus made such a perfect job, I do not need the glasses I had before I was ill, and I am now writing dozens of letters a day! To Him be all the glory!

The Welsh lady who sent me this testimony informed me in her letter that Margery Steven was still alive and well.

I sat at my desk, stunned. It wasn't coincidence. In God's marvelous providence, someone had sent my book to this lady at just the right time so that she would send to me at just the right time a copy of this testimony. Here I was, writing the very words to undermine people's faith in God's willingness to heal today, when the letter arrived from someone I'd never met!

God was determined to put some sense into a preacher's head and some passion into his heart. It worked!

The Gift of Faith

Before I say anything more about healing, a few words about the gift of faith are in order. Although the New Testament has much to say about faith in general, it doesn't explicitly refer to the *charisma*, or gift, of faith outside the passage in 1 Corinthians 12. Therefore, the best way to identify and define the nature of this gift is to see how faith is portrayed elsewhere. The New Testament mentions three distinct ways in which faith is exercised: *conversion faith*, *continuing faith*, and *charismatic faith*.

Conversion faith is the faith through which we are justified. This is the trust or belief in the atoning sacrifice of Christ at conversion. Paul referred to this faith in Ephesians 2:8–9 (emphasis added): "By grace you have been saved *through faith*; and this is not of yourselves, it is the gift of God; not as a result of works, so that no one may boast" (see also Romans 1:16–17; 3:28; 5:1). Unlike the *gift* of faith, which is restricted to those believers to whom the Spirit wills to give it (see 1 Corinthians 12:11), every Christian has this kind of faith.

Continuing faith is the faith we exercise daily as we look confidently to God to do in and through our lives all He has promised to do. This faith is one of the fruits of the Spirit (see Galatians 5:22) and is the faith of Hebrews 11 (compared with 1 Peter 1:8 and other passages). All believers have this faith, but some are more confident in the goodness and greatness of God in daily life.

Charismatic faith is the faith that is spontaneous, a God-enabled condition in which the supernatural actions of God take place. This, I believe, is the "gift of faith" in 1 Corinthians 12:9. Consider these examples of the gift of faith:

And Jesus answered and said to them, "Have faith in God. Truly I say to you, whoever says to this mountain, 'Be taken up and thrown into the sea,' and does not doubt in his heart, but believes that what he says is going to happen, it will be granted to him. Therefore, I say to you, all things for which you pray and ask, believe that you have received them, and they will be granted to you."

Mark 11:22–24 (see also Matthew 17:20–21; 21:21–22)

And the prayer of faith will restore the one who is sick, and the Lord will raise him up, and if he has committed sins, they will be forgiven him.

James 5:15

It seems that any believer can experience this manifestation of the Spirit, a faith which enables a believer to trust God to bring about certain things for which there is not a divine promise from Scripture, beyond what one normally imagines. The gift of faith is a surge of confidence that rises in a particular need or challenge and assures a person that God is about to act.

Linking Faith and Healing

In Paul's list of the gifts, the gifts of healings and miracles are bound up with the gift of faith, which is listed just before them.

The role of faith in healing is crucial. Sometimes, the faith of the person needing healing is instrumental (see Matthew 9:22); other times, it is the faith of a friend or family member (see Matthew 15:28; Mark 2:5, 11). Sometimes, it's the faith of the person praying for the one who needs healing (see Mark 9:17–24); other times, faith may not play a part in the healing at all (see John 5:1–9, where John never mentions faith as a condition for healing; see also Matthew 8:14). God may simply heal by His sovereign act, unrelated to anything in us. But often, Jesus healed because of someone's faith.

In the cases of both Jairus and the woman suffering from bleeding in Mark 5, faith was directed toward Jesus. Again, in Luke 17:11–19, Jesus healed ten lepers. When one returned to say thanks, Jesus said, "Your faith has made you well" (verse 19). When Bartimaeus asked Jesus to heal him of his blindness, Jesus said, "Go . . . your faith has healed you" (Mark 10:52 NIV). In the story of the paralytic being lowered through the roof, Jesus healed the man when He saw the faith of the man's friends (see again Mark 2:5).

Faith for Healing

I believe faith for healing operates in a believer at any one of the following five levels.

1. Faith that God is your *sole source* for blessing, your only hope (see Psalm 33:18–22; 147:10–11). Faith points us away from ourselves, our power, and our resources, to God. Faith says, "Lord, I am nothing, and You are everything. I entrust myself to Your care. My confidence is in Your word and character."

   Faith is an act of self-denial, renouncing one's ability to do anything—and a confession that God can do everything. Faith's power comes not from the spiritual energy of the person who believes, but from the power of God! It is not faith's *act*, but its *object* that accounts for the miraculous.

2. Faith in God's *ability* to heal. Jesus took special delight in healing those who were receptive to and trusted in His power. In Matthew 9:28–29, Jesus asked the two blind men if they believed that He was able to heal them. He wanted to know if they trusted His ability. "Yes, Lord," came their response (verse 28). Jesus replied, "It shall be done for you according to your faith" (verse 29), and they

were instantly healed. Jesus regarded their confidence in His power to help them as "faith" and healed them on that basis.

"Jesus, I believe You are able to heal me" is faith that pleases Him. I can almost hear Jesus say, "Yes! I was waiting to hear you say that. It's important that you truly believe I am capable of doing this." The hemorrhaging woman was healed when she simply touched Jesus' garment. "Your faith has healed you," Jesus told her (Mark 5:34 NIV). In other words, "I respond to your confidence and trust in My ability."

3. Faith in God's *desire* to heal—faith in His goodness and desire to bless His children (see Psalm 103; Luke 11:11–13). This is confidence in God's character to build up, not tear down; to bring unity, not division; to create wholeness, not disintegration. Every time Jesus healed, we see His care and compassion. People came to Jesus for healing because they knew He would understand their pain, their frustration. Their healing flowed from their personal encounter with a loving Person. Jesus embodied compassion and power.

4. Faith that God *does* heal. This is the faith that healing is part of God's purpose and plan for His people today. You can believe that God is able to heal and delights to heal, yet not believe that healing is for the Church today. For example, I believe that God can make manna fall from heaven to feed His people and that He delights in providing food. But I do not have faith that God intends to send manna from heaven as a means of providing for our physical needs today. Therefore, I will not spend time praying that He do so.

5. Faith that it is His will to heal *right now*. This is the certainty that healing is what God is, in fact, going to

do now. This is probably more of what Paul had in mind when he spoke of the gift of faith in 1 Corinthians 12:9. It may also be what James referred to as "the prayer offered in faith" (James 5:15 NIV).

The prayer of faith isn't one that we pray whenever we want to. It is a unique prayer, divinely energized only on those occasions when God is about to impart a gift for healing. In the original, James was careful to place the definite article "the" before both prayer and faith (hence, "the prayer offered in the faith"). One prays this prayer only when prompted by Spirit-wrought conviction that God intends to heal the one for whom the prayer is being offered.

This is more than merely believing that God can heal; this is faith that *in this case*, He is willing to heal, and heal now. God sovereignly bestows this faith. When God chooses to heal, He produces in the heart(s) of those praying faith that healing is His intent. The kind of faith to which James refers, in response to which God heals, is not the kind that we exercise at *our* will, but when *God* wills.

One Sunday, a couple came to me and asked that the elders of our church anoint their infant son and pray for his healing. Later, we gathered in the back room and I anointed him with oil. He was only two weeks old and had been diagnosed with a serious liver disorder that could require surgery, perhaps even a transplant, if something didn't change.

As we prayed, something very unusual happened. As we laid hands on this young child, I found myself suddenly filled with an overwhelming confidence that he would be healed. Not wanting to be presumptuous, I tried to doubt, but couldn't. I prayed confidently, filled with an unshakable faith. I said silently to God, *Lord, You really are going to heal him!* Although the family left the room unsure, I was certain God had healed him. The next morning, the doctor agreed. The baby was totally healed, and is healthy and happy today.

The Prayer of Faith

Let's look at James 5 again. James made several key points about the relationship of sickness to sin in verse 15: "and the prayer of faith will restore the one who is sick, and the Lord will raise him up, and if he [the sick man] has committed sins, they will be forgiven him." James is in harmony with Jesus and Paul that not all sickness is the result of sin (see John 9:1–3; 2 Corinthians 12:1–10). Sometimes it is the result of sin (see 1 Corinthians 11:27–30; Mark 2:1–12), but not always. If sin were responsible for someone's sickness, God healing that person physically showed that God forgave his or her sin as well.

Perhaps the sin James had in mind was bitterness, resentment, jealousy, or unforgiveness. So, James advised us to "confess your sins to one another" (James 5:16). He probably had in mind either confessing to a person against whom you have sinned, or confessing to another believer. What this tells us is that *God connects healing mercy to the repentance of His people.* When the hurting are not healed, it may be due to stubbornness or spiritual insensitivity more than to "God doesn't heal anymore."

Finally, take careful note of the example of Elijah and the rain (see James 5:17–18). James wanted his readers to know that Elijah was just like us—human, with weaknesses, fears, doubts, and failures. James said, in effect, "Elijah wasn't extraordinary. So, pray the way he did!" And don't forget the context: James appealed to the example of Elijah to encourage us *when we pray for the sick!* The point is that we should pray for miraculous healing with the same faith and expectation with which Elijah prayed for the end of a three-year drought.

It's Not a Single Gift?

Remember my opening statement that there is no such thing as the gift of healing? I said this both because of the way Paul described this spiritual phenomenon and the misconceptions surrounding it. The significant point about verses 9 and 28 in 1 Corinthians 12 is that both *gifts* and *healings* are plural and lack the definite article, hence the translation "gifts of healings." Paul did not seem to envision a person endowed with one healing gift for all diseases. His language suggests many different gifts of healing, each *appropriate to and effective for* its related illness, and each occurrence of healing constituting a distinct gift.

I've often met people who have what appears to be a healing anointing for one specific affliction. Some pray more effectively for those with back problems, while others see healings when praying for migraine headaches. This may be what Paul had in mind when he spoke of "gifts of healings."

For a proper understanding of healing, eliminate the wrong assumption that if God ever healed through a person, that person would *always* see healings come through him or her. But look at Paul: In view of the lingering illness of Epaphroditus (see Philippians 2:25–30), Timothy (see 1 Timothy 5:23), Trophimus (see 2 Timothy 4:20), and perhaps Paul himself (see 2 Corinthians 12:7–10; Galatians 4:13), let's view this gift as subject to the will of God, not of people. Few doubt that Paul had a gift for healing, but his prayers for Epaphroditus weren't answered, at least not at first. Timothy and Trophimus were not immediately healed either. Clearly, Paul could not heal at will. Aside from Jesus, no one else could either! And there is doubt if even Jesus could (see John 5:19; Mark 6:5–6).

So when people say, "I don't have the gift of healing," according to my reading of Paul, there is no such thing as a God-given ability to heal everyone of every disease on every occasion.

Rather, the Spirit sovereignly distributes a charisma of healing for a particular need. "Gifts of healings" are occasional and subject to the sovereign purposes of God.

Healing is an expression of divine mercy (see Philippians 2:27), never to be viewed as a right. God does not owe us healing. We should have faith for healing. But there is a vast difference between faith in divine mercy and presumption based on a "right."

The word *mercy* is the same one used in the gospels to describe why Jesus healed people while He was on the earth. God's motive for healing hasn't changed! God healed through Jesus prior to Pentecost because He is a merciful, compassionate God. God continues to heal after Pentecost because He is a merciful, compassionate God.

We're More Than a Spirit

Some in the Church today disregard healing because they believe that to focus on physical health and well-being is misguided, and that our attention is to be focused on the condition of our souls. But this comes close to a version of ancient Gnosticism. Among the many beliefs of ancient Gnostics was the belief that the physical body is not God's good creation, but is evil, as is *all matter*. Gnostics tended to one of two extremes as a result of this belief. Some deprived the body, treating it harshly through fasting and self-flagellation, while others indulged the body in sensual pleasure such as promiscuous sex and excessive food and drink.

But the biblical view of the body is that *God created us*. We are both material and immaterial (see Genesis 2:7). Christ redeemed *our bodies* no less than our souls, and they are the temple of the Holy Spirit (see 1 Corinthians 6:19–20).

Our bodies are designed "for the Lord" (1 Corinthians 6:13) and are to be used to honor God (see verse 20). Our bodies will be resurrected and glorified. At the Judgment Seat of Christ, we will account for what we did while in our bodies. Spirituality is also physical. When God created us in His image, He gave us bodies. Although God is Spirit, He created the entire physical world and called it *good* (see Genesis 1:4, 12, 18, 21, 25).

Let's Recap

Here are several important observations that I hope will encourage you to take your hands out of your pockets, fix your faith on the grace and power of God, and pray regularly for the sick. First, healing and health are always portrayed in Scripture as the blessing of God. While God uses sickness to discipline and instruct us, sickness itself is never portrayed as His blessing (see Psalms 6:2–3, 6–7; 32:1–7; 38; 41:1–4; 88:1–9, 15–18; 102:1–5, 8–11; 119:67, 71, 75).

Second, although sickness is suffering, not all suffering is sickness. Jesus promised that all who follow Him would suffer persecution, slander, and rejection—but He never said that about sickness.

Third, sickness and disease, in and of themselves, do not glorify God—but our unwavering faith and love for God *in spite of* sickness and disease *do* glorify Him.

Fourth, we must leave room for mystery. God's ways are beyond us. We can't expect to understand why some are sick and others not, or why some are healed and others not. But the fact that many are not healed should never justify *not* praying for them!

Fifth, God's heart is for healing, not hurting. My working assumption is that God's heart is for healing. Continue to pray for the sick until God tells you otherwise, or until they die!

Sixth, there is no "failure." We *succeed* whenever we *obey* the Scriptures to pray for the sick. Whether they are healed, and how they are healed, rests with God.

Although many say they believe that God still heals today, they live as if He won't. They rarely or never lay hands on the sick and pray with any expectancy, sometimes because they confuse praying *expectantly* with praying *presumptuously*. Prayer is presumptuous only when the person claims healing without revelation, or makes the unbiblical assumption that God *always* wills to heal then and there. They then feel required to account for the absence of healing by appealing to a deficiency of faith (usually in the one for whom prayer is offered).

Pray expectantly. Humbly petition a merciful God for something we don't deserve, but that He delights to give (see Luke 11:9–13; see also Matthew 9:27–31; 20:29–34; Luke 17:13–14). Expectant prayer flows from the recognition that Jesus healed people because He loved them and felt compassion for them (see Matthew 14:13–14; 20:34; Mark 1:41–42; Luke 7:11–17), which is the disposition of the heart of God. Nothing in Scripture indicates that His heart has changed!

FIVE

It's a Miracle!

Is it okay to pray for a miracle? For years, I thought it was unspiritual to desire *any* spiritual gifts, especially miraculous ones. I had been taught that to seek signs indicated weak faith and ignorance. Only *those* people prayed for healing or a miracle. But then I noticed Acts 4:29–31, the prayer of the Jerusalem church:

> "And now, Lord, take note of their threats, and grant it to Your bond-servants to speak Your word with all confidence, while You extend Your hand to heal, and signs and wonders take place through the name of Your holy servant Jesus." And when they had prayed, the place where they had gathered together was shaken, and they were all filled with the Holy Spirit and began to speak the word of God with boldness.

Evidently, *these believers* didn't see any inconsistency between miracles and the message of the Gospel! Jesus did rebuke as wicked those who craved and sought after signs, because they were unbelieving leaders who wanted to justify their unbelief and refusal to follow Jesus (see Matthew 12:39; 16:4; compare to 1 Corinthians 1:22).

If our prayers for power are born of a desire to see God glorified and His people healed, I hardly think Jesus would respond to us as He did the religious leaders of His day. When a passion for miraculous gifts is prompted *not* by a selfish hankering for the sensational, but by compassion for diseased and despairing souls, God cannot help but be pleased.

Doing the Works of Jesus

One of the most amazing things Jesus ever said is found in John 14:12: "Truly, truly, I say to you, the one who believes in Me, the works that I do, he will do also; and greater works than these he will do; *because I am going to the Father*" (emphasis added). This statement confuses most of us. The question is, How do you respond to your confusion? I believe there are only three options:

1. Reject the statement, and believe that the Bible contains error.
2. Interpret Jesus' words in the light of how *my experience* does not measure up to His claims. (I held this position for years.)
3. Receive Jesus' words, and trust God to sort out the confusion as we seek to pray for their fulfillment!

Jesus described a person who performed these works as "the one who believes in Me." This Greek phrase in John's gospel always refers to any person who trusts in Christ, whether apostle or average follower (see John 3:15–16, 18, 36; 6:35, 40, 47; 7:38; 11:25–26; 12:44, 46; 14:12). It never refers solely to the apostles.

Second, the works Jesus said believers would do may well be *more* than miracles and healings, but they are certainly not

44

less than miracles and healings. The immediately preceding verse says, "Believe Me that I am in the Father and the Father is in Me; otherwise believe because of the works themselves" (John 14:11). If one was to believe in Jesus "because of" certain "works" He did, then they were visible and unavoidable. Those miracles were the basis upon which Jesus called people to believe.

Jesus attributed the ability of His followers to do His works to the fact that He was going "to the Father." In the context of John 13–17, this points us to the gift of the Holy Spirit given after Jesus' ascension (see John 14:16, 26; 15:26; 16:7).

The Gift of Miracles

The most literal translation of Paul's words in 1 Corinthians 12:10 is "workings of powers" (*energemata dunameon*). Although all gifts are "workings" (*energemata*) or "energizings" by divine power (compare to verses 6 and 11), the word is used here in conjunction with "powers" (*dunamis*) for a specific gift. The word often translated "miracles" in 1 Corinthians 12:10 is the Greek word for powers (*dunamis*). Thus, we again have a double plural, "workings of powers," which probably points to variety in these operations.

Several possible manifestations of divine power may be included in what Paul means by "workings of powers" or "miracles." Consider the following:

Acts 9:40, where Peter raised Tabitha/Dorcas from the dead (although even this is a healing in the strictest sense of the term).

Acts 13:8–11, where Paul induced blindness on Elymas. One might also include here Peter's word of disciplinary judgment that resulted in the immediate death of Ananias and Sapphira (see Acts 5:1–11).

Miracles such as turning water to wine, stilling the storm on the Sea of Galilee, producing food, and supernatural deliverances (exorcisms) also fall into this category.

Defining a Miracle

The word *miracle* describes everything from healing a paralytic to finding a parking space at the mall on the day before Christmas. What is a good, biblical working definition of a miracle?

1. Jesus said a miracle is proof that the Kingdom of God has come upon us (see Matthew 12:28).
2. It is surprising and unexplainable (except for the power of God).
3. It is something only God can do.
4. It often may have symbolic or "sign" value (some aspect that points to God's character or agenda on earth).

Because many Christians see God as uninvolved in their lives, they ignore passages that assert God's immediate involvement in everything from the growth of a blade of grass (see Psalm 104) to the sustaining of our very lives (see Acts 17; Colossians 1:17).

God, who is always and everywhere present, upholding and sustaining and directing all things to their appointed end, is now working in a surprising and unfamiliar way. This also helps us answer the question of whether unusual answers to prayer are miracles. I would say yes—anytime such answers arouse awe, wonder, and acknowledgment of God's power (e.g., 1 Kings 18:24, 36–38; Acts 12:5–17; 28:8).

Jesus the Healer

Jesus' first goal was to come as the Lamb of God who takes away the sin of the world. But to show humans who God is,

Jesus delivered individuals from pain and poverty and demons and distress. His death on the cross is the foundation for the ultimate removal of pain from His people, whether that happens now or in heaven. Jesus ascended to heaven so that He might send the Spirit and we might do the very works of healing and deliverance and mercy and miracles that He Himself did (see again John 14:12).

I'm not saying that all pain will disappear prior to Christ's return. Even then, Jesus came to give us an example of how to bear up under it if we are not healed and delivered from it (see 2 Corinthians 12:7–10 about Paul's "thorn in the flesh"). We should pray for healing and deliverance from pain, confident that our loving heavenly Father delights in glorifying His Son by ministering to us in mercy and compassion. But if, for reasons beyond our understanding, the Father chooses instead to give us grace and strength to endure pain as we await His Son from heaven, so be it.

Many Christians are confused about how miracles relate to the Gospel. They are afraid that praying for miracles neglects the Gospel. But Paul, who described his gospel ministry as characterized by the "power of signs and wonders, in the power of the [Holy] Spirit" (Romans 15:19), was the same man who declared that "the word of the cross" is the power of God to salvation (1 Corinthians 1:18). He said, "I determined to know nothing among you except Jesus Christ, and Him crucified" (1 Corinthians 2:2), but also preached that truth "not in persuasive words of wisdom, but in demonstration of the Spirit and of power" (verse 4). Paul reminded the Thessalonians that the Gospel did not come to them "in word only, but also in power and in the Holy Spirit and with full conviction" (1 Thessalonians 1:5). If any generation in the history of the Church knew the power of preaching and the authentication of the Gospel from firsthand evidence of the resurrection, it was this one. Yet they prayed passionately for God to bring signs and wonders.

Others have argued that any focus on the power of spiritual gifts ignores a call to suffer for the Gospel. Those who desire and pray for the miraculous, they say, ignore the reality that afflictions, persecution, and suffering are an inevitable part of living in the "not yet" of the Kingdom. But Paul certainly sensed no incompatibility between the two; they both characterized his life and ministry. The miracles in the Holy Spirit's ministry through Paul were performed in a world of distress and slander and heartache in which he suffered as an obedient servant of Christ.

Miracles do not always produce saving faith in those who witness them, but that's not because of a fault in the miracle or because miracles are wrong. It is simply because people are hard-hearted and spiritually blind. The fact is, miracles often lead to great evangelistic success (see John 5:36; 10:25, 37–38; 12:9–11; 14:11; 20:30–31; Acts 8:4–8; 9:32–43; Romans 15:18–19) and can be a tremendous boost to our faith in the power and compassion of God (see 1 Corinthians 14:3). These are all signs (as Jesus said) that the Kingdom has come upon us! And remember that Paul said God gave all supernatural phenomena—healings, tongues, prophecy, even miracles—to the Church "for the common good" (1 Corinthians 12:7).

What about forgiveness of sin? I think it was easier for Jesus to speak the words "your sins are forgiven" because no man could *see* whether they were forgiven or not. But if He said the words "rise and walk," observers *could* see the paralyzed person walk (see Mark 2:1–12). Jesus' point was to prove that He had the *invisible* power to forgive sins by demonstrating the *visible* power to heal a paralyzed man. Jesus Himself declared, "But so that you may know that the Son of Man has authority on earth to forgive sins . . . I say to you, get up, pick up your pallet, and go home" (verses 10–11).

John 10:37–38 gives us simply one example of the challenge Jesus issued to the Pharisees: "If I do not do the works of

My Father, do not believe Me; but if I do them, though you do not believe Me, *believe the works*, so that you may know and understand that the Father is in Me, and I in the Father" (emphasis added).

Are miracles the cure-all for society's ills and the Church's problems? Of course not. *Jesus is*. But the Jesus who entered society and ministered to its ills, who created the Church and is its saving Lord, is a miracle-working Jesus. And if God should equip us to minister in the miraculous, we should humbly offer ourselves to Him as His hands and feet.

SIX

Prophecy and Distinguishing of Spirits

A former student of mine was going through a difficult season in her life. God seemed far away, her job was unfulfilling, and she thought about pursuing a different line of work. She certainly didn't expect that at a conference, a man widely known for his prophetic gift would ask her to stand.

As the man gave her words of encouragement, along with some advice drawn from a biblical text he thought was relevant to her life, he paused and said, "I just saw the number 202 above your head. I believe that is where you work." He then continued.

I was closely watching this student and noticed her initial confusion when he mentioned 202. About thirty seconds later, though, she realized what he had said. I later asked her, "What happened?"

She said, "When he identified 202 as the place I worked, I thought he was giving the street address. My first reaction was that he had missed it. But then it dawned on me that 202 is the number of my office suite!"

I've seen a prophetic word work this way often—at just the right time in a person's life, at that moment when there is a need to know that God is near, that He cares, that He still loves and guides and answers prayer. There is simply no way to explain this information as a lucky guess; it either came from the devil to deceive and destroy my student's confidence in God, or it came from the Holy Spirit to edify and console her (see 1 Corinthians 14:3).

When I use the word *prophecy*, I do not mean the prediction of future events. Unfortunately, it has come to be associated almost exclusively in the minds of many with something about the end times. When I use the word *prophecy*, I mean the spiritual gift Paul described in 1 Corinthians 12–14 and elsewhere in the New Testament. A simple definition of prophecy is "the human report of a divine revelation." Prophecy is speaking forth in human words something God has spontaneously brought to the speaker's mind.

In all our talk of prophecy and the stories we tell, we tend to neglect the principles and guidelines set forth by the apostle Paul in 1 Corinthians 14 for this gift. Much of the error into which people fall through the misuse of this gift could be remedied by carefully examining all Paul says in this important chapter. Let's make a short study of 1 Corinthians 14. Please read this section with an open Bible. My selected insights seek to answer several questions about the nature and function of the prophetic gift.

Is It Okay to Pursue Prophecy?

It's not only okay to pursue prophecy, but also mandatory! In 1 Corinthians 14:1, Paul commanded us to desire earnestly spiritual gifts, "especially that you may prophesy."

Again in 1 Corinthians 14:39, Paul exhorted us to "earnestly desire to prophesy."

In 1 Corinthians 14:12, Paul wrote, "So you too, since you are eager to possess spiritual gifts [referring to his readers' enthusiasm for tongues], strive to excel for the edification of the church [the gift of prophecy, according to the context]."

Paul was not merely suggesting that prophecy is a good gift. He was *commanding* that we earnestly desire to exercise this gift in the local Body.

Paul's words leave us little room for waffling! He says, in effect, "If you are not earnestly desiring to prophesy, if you are not praying for opportunity and occasion to speak prophetically into the lives of other believers, you are disobeying God!"

Could Anyone Prophesy?

Yes, any believer could prophesy, but that doesn't mean every believer should expect to function *consistently* as a prophet in the Church. Paul wished that "all" would prophesy (see 1 Corinthians 14:5), but does that mean he expected them to? His desire for people to prophesy came from his recognition that the "one who prophesies edifies the church" (1 Corinthians 14:4).

In two other places, Paul seemed to envision the possibility that any Christian might speak prophetically (see verses 24, 31). But again, this doesn't mean that everyone will prophesy. He was probably drawing a distinction between people who consistently prophesy with ease and accuracy with those who prophesy occasionally.

Let's not forget Peter's quotation in Acts 2 of Joel's prophecy. The result of this pouring out of the Spirit is that "your sons and your daughters will prophesy" (verse 17). The characteristic feature of this present age is the revelatory activity of the Spirit (dreams and visions), which forms the basis for prophetic utterance. Not all will be prophets, but it appears that all may prophesy (see Ephesians 4:11; 1 Corinthians 12:29).

What Does God Reveal in Prophecy?

In 1 Corinthians 14:25, Paul described prophecy as disclosing the "secrets" of the heart. I have seen this often. People who believed their thoughts, fantasies, sins, and plans were hidden from God are shocked by the revelations of His Spirit. Paul describes in this same verse only one way for such a person to respond to the prophetic gift: "He will fall on his face and worship God, declaring that God is certainly among you."

I referred earlier to Charles Spurgeon (1834–1892), widely regarded as one of the greatest preachers ever. His life was an example of godliness and zeal, and his ministry was characterized by a commitment to the authority of Scripture. Although Spurgeon deeply depended on the power of the Holy Spirit in his ministry, he was not known for advocating miraculous gifts in the Church. Yet Spurgeon himself experienced what can only be regarded as prophetic revelation. Although he did not refer to it as revelation, that does not change the reality of it! The following incidents are taken directly from Spurgeon's autobiography. You judge whether or not they are expressions of the gifting described by the apostle Paul in 1 Corinthians 14:24–25.

> While preaching in the hall, on one occasion, I deliberately pointed to a man in the crowd, and said, "There is a man sitting there, who is a shoemaker; he keeps his shop open on Sundays, it was open last Sabbath morning, he took ninepence, and there was fourpence profit out of it; his soul is sold to Satan for fourpence!" A city missionary, when going his rounds, met with this man, and seeing that he was reading one of my sermons, he asked the question, "Do you know Mr. Spurgeon?" "Yes," replied the man, "I have every reason to know him, I have been to hear him; and, under his preaching, by God's grace I have become a new creature in Christ Jesus. Shall I tell you how it happened? I went to the Music Hall, and

took my seat in the middle of the place; Mr. Spurgeon looked at me as if he knew me, and in his sermon he pointed to me, and told the congregation that I was a shoemaker, and that I kept my shop open on Sundays; and I did, sir. I should not have minded that; but he also said that I took ninepence the Sunday before, and that there was fourpence profit out of it. I did take ninepence that day, and fourpence was just the profit; but how he should know that, I could not tell. Then it struck me that it was God who had spoken to my soul through him, so I shut up my shop the next Sunday. At first, I was afraid to go again to hear him, lest he should tell the people more about me; but afterwards I went, and the Lord met with me, and saved my soul."[1]

Spurgeon then added:

I could tell as many as a dozen similar cases in which I pointed at somebody in the hall without having the slightest knowledge of the person, or any idea that what I said was right, except that I believed I was moved by the Spirit to say it; and so striking has been my description, that the persons have gone away, and said to their friends, "Come, see a man that told me all things that ever I did; beyond a doubt, he must have been sent of God to my soul, or else he could not have described me so exactly." And not only so, but I have known many instances in which the thoughts of men have been revealed from the pulpit. I have sometimes seen persons nudge their neighbours with their elbow, because they had got a smart hit, and they have been heard to say, when they were going out, "The preacher told us just what we said to one another when we went in at the door."[2]

Spurgeon made no explicit reference to miraculous gifts such as prophecy and the word of knowledge. But Spurgeon's own testimony describes these well!

Where Does Prophecy Come From?

All prophecy is based on revelation. In 1 Corinthians 14:30, Paul wrote, "If a revelation is made to another who is seated, then the first one is to keep silent" (see also verse 26). In 1 Corinthians 13:2, Paul seems to suggest that prophecies are based on the reception of divine "mysteries." The verb "to reveal" (*apokalupto*) occurs 26 times in the New Testament, and the noun "revelation" occurs 18 times. In every instance the reference is to divine activity, never to human communication.

Prophecy is never based on a hunch, a supposition, an inference, an educated guess, or even sanctified wisdom. Prophecy is the human report of a *divine revelation*. This is what distinguishes prophecy from teaching. Teaching is always based on a text of Scripture. Prophecy is always based on a spontaneous revelation.

Although rooted in revelation, prophecy is occasionally fallible. I know what you're thinking: *How can God reveal something that contains error? How can the infallible God reveal something that is fallible?* The answer is simple: He can't. He doesn't. Every prophecy has three elements; only one is assuredly God. First is God's disclosure to a human. Second is the interpretation of what has been disclosed. Third is the application of that interpretation.

God alone is responsible for the revelation. Whatever He discloses to the human mind is wholly free from error. It is as infallible as God is, true in all its parts. Indeed, the revelation that is the root of every genuine prophetic utterance is as inerrant and infallible as the written Word of God itself (the Bible).

The problem is, *you* might misinterpret or misapply what God has disclosed! The fact that God has spoken perfectly doesn't mean that you have *heard* perfectly. It is possible for a person to interpret and apply, without error, what God has revealed. But God's revelation does not in itself *guarantee* that the interpretation or application will be perfect.

This troubles some, and leads them to conclude that all New Testament prophecy is of no benefit to the Church. After all, how can a gift that is potentially fallible bless anyone? To put your fears to rest, let's next compare prophecy with the gift of teaching.

Prophecy and Teaching

Imagine: Your pastor is teaching on the book of 1 Thessalonians. Each week, he has before him the revealed, inspired, written Word of God, from which he draws his comments. He has come to chapter 4, where Paul discusses the Rapture of the Church. He tells you that, after careful study and prayer, he believes the Rapture will occur before the Tribulation.

Later, you're chatting with a friend who insists that the Rapture occurs at the midpoint of the Tribulation. You, on the other hand, are persuaded that the Rapture won't come until *after* the Tribulation. What's going on? All three of you are reading the same Bible (even the same translation). Each of you has been diligent in studying the same passage. Each of you has prayed for Holy Spirit illumination. Yet, three people walk away with three conflicting interpretations and differing applications.

So, should you denounce teaching and insist that a gift so obviously susceptible to error and abuse be banned? Of course not. You've been blessed by the sermons and are excited about what God is doing in your life. You realize that only the Bible has intrinsic authority. What your pastor says, in the exercise of his spiritual gift, has authority *only* in a secondary sense. He may have come up short in his interpretation or application, but that's no reason to repudiate the spiritual gift of teaching!

Like teaching, prophecy is also based on a revelation from God. In some way beyond ordinary perception, God reveals something to the mind of the prophet that is not found in Scripture (but is never contrary to it). The revelation, having come from God, is true and error free. Like the Bible, it alone has divine authority. But the gift of prophecy does not guarantee the infallible *transmission* of that revelation. The prophet may perceive imperfectly, may understand imperfectly, or may communicate imperfectly (not unlike what happened with your pastor and his exposition of 1 Thessalonians 4).

That is why Paul says that "we see in a mirror dimly" (1 Corinthians 13:12). The gift of prophecy may result in fallible prophecy, just as the gift of teaching may result in fallible teaching. Therefore, if teaching (a gift prone to fallibility) can edify and build up the Church, why can't prophecy be good for edifying it as well (see 1 Corinthians 14:3, 12, 26)? Even though both gifts suffer from human imperfection and require testing, they build up the Body.

How Does Revelation Come?

The way in which a revelation comes is not specified. An audible voice, a vision, words, thoughts, or perhaps mental pictures impress themselves upon the mind and spirit.

Remember the story I told about my student and the number 202? A similar incident occurred in the same meeting a few moments later. The same man was speaking to a couple about their call to evangelism. He said, "I just saw a picture of a young boy dressed up like General MacArthur. I'll just bet that your son's name is Douglas." Sure enough, they have a boy named Douglas.

This may strike you as a bizarre way for God to communicate to someone. I can only suggest that you read your Bible again to notice how often God does incredibly bizarre and strange things, at least by Western standards!

But how does a prophet know that what he or she is receiving is from the Holy Spirit rather than from some other source? A related and more important question is, How do the *rest of us* know? I'll answer this in the next chapter.

Do Prophets Lose Control?

Paul never teaches that a loss of control, ecstasy, or a trance-like state is part of prophecy. Several factors support this conclusion:

1. Paul assumed that the person prophesying could recognize that someone else had received a revelation and was ready to speak. Clearly, the prophets were also expected to cease speaking upon recognition that another person had received a revelation (1 Corinthians 14:30, "then the first one is to keep silent"). The prophet could both speak and keep silent at will. Also, the second prophet waited until the first one had stopped.

2. Paul said that all who prophesied could do so in turn, "one by one" (verse 31), indicating that they had voluntary control of themselves. Paul goes on to say that "the spirits of prophets are subject to prophets" (verse 32). He was referring to the many different manifestations of the one Holy Spirit through the spirit of each individual prophet (see also verses 12, 14–16). This means that the Holy Spirit will never force a prophet to speak, but voluntarily submits to the prophet's timing for the sake of order. This isn't a declaration that we are more powerful than the Holy Spirit. It's that the Holy Spirit is gentle—some call Him "a Gentleman." It isn't the nature of the Spirit to incite confusion or to coerce people. The Spirit is neither impetuous nor uncontrollable.

Did Paul Allow Women to Prophesy?

I believe women can and should prophesy. In Peter's speech on the Day of Pentecost, he explicitly said that the Spirit imparts prophetic gifts to both men and women:

> "And it shall be in the last days," God says, "that I will pour out My Spirit on all mankind; and your sons and your daughters will prophesy, and your young men will see visions, and your old men will have dreams; and even on My male and female servants I will pour out My Spirit in those days, and they will prophesy."
>
> Acts 2:17–18

In Acts 21:9, Luke referred to Philip's four daughters as having the gift of prophecy. And in 1 Corinthians 11:5, Paul gave instructions regarding how women were to pray and prophesy in a church meeting.

In that light, what did Paul mean when he wrote, "The women are to keep silent in the churches; for they are not permitted to speak" (1 Corinthians 14:34)? I want to mention two most likely views. Here is the first:

1. Paul prohibits women from participating in the passing of judgment upon or the evaluation of the prophecies (see 1 Corinthians 14:29). In other words, Paul is not imposing absolute silence on all women. Rather he is calling for silence only in one regard, namely, the public evaluation of prophetic utterances.

We should note that Paul has already imposed silence twice before in this very paragraph, and in neither case is the silence absolute. First, in verse 28 he tells those who speak in tongues to remain "silent" if there is no interpreter. But surely, they could speak in other ways during worship. Second, in verse 30

60

he tells those who were prophesying to remain "silent" if someone else received a revelation. Again, no one believes that these two demands for "silence" mean that such people could never open their mouths again during worship!

There are contextual considerations on the command "to be silent" (*sigao*). Someone is to be silent while someone else is speaking (see Acts 12:17; 15:12–13; 1 Corinthians 14:30). The one who is silent does not speak in a certain manner or on a certain topic, but he or she can speak in other ways and on other issues. Thus, in this view, Paul would be restricting speech designed to critique prophetic utterances, but would not be prohibiting other forms of speaking.

This view is supported by the structure of 1 Corinthians 14:27–28. When Paul advises on tongues, he first restricts the number who can speak to "by two or at the most three," and then he gives instruction to ensure that the congregation will be edified "each one in turn, and one is to interpret; but if there is no interpreter, he is to keep silent in church; and have him speak to himself and to God."

Then, in verse 29 Paul turns to the issue of prophecy and first restricts the number who can prophesy to "two or three," and then ensures that the congregation will be edified by insisting that the others should pass judgment.

In verses 30–35, Paul addresses the issues he raised in verse 29. In verses 30–33, he takes up the first part of verse 29, "let two or three prophets speak." In verses 33–35, he takes up the second part, "and let the others weigh what is said" (ESV). If this outline is correct, Paul would be forbidding women to speak in church only regarding the evaluation of prophetic utterances. Evidently, he believed that this was an exercise of authority only for men (see 1 Timothy 2:12–15).

If we assume that in 1 Timothy 2 Paul prohibits women from teaching or exercising authority over men, it is understandable why he would allow women to prophesy in 1 Corinthians 11:5, but forbid them from judging the prophetic utterances of others (especially men) in 1 Corinthians 14:34.

This view also explains Paul's appeal to "the Law" (i.e., the Old Testament) in verse 34. The Old Testament does not teach that women are to remain silent at all times in worship (see Exodus 15:20–21; 2 Samuel 6:15, 19; Psalm 148:12), but it does endorse male headship in the home and in worship, consistent with Paul's teaching here and elsewhere.

The second view about what Paul meant by women keeping silent is this:

2. When Paul tells women to "keep silent," he is not prohibiting them from making a verbal contribution to the meeting, whether in the form of worship or praying or prophesying or reading Scripture or sharing a testimony. Rather, Paul is prohibiting women from engaging in the public questioning of another woman's husband. There are two primary reasons why this makes sense. In verse 35, Paul says that the women's speaking was motivated by a desire to "learn." The "speaking" Paul silences was their asking questions to gain insight. If they want to learn, and it is perfectly right and good that they should, they must wait and ask their husbands at home. Note well: Paul does not say, "If they have something to contribute, they should tell their husbands later at home," but rather, "If they desire to learn anything, let them ask their own husbands at home."

Why would it be inappropriate for women in a church meeting to ask questions in their pursuit of knowledge? The answer is found in the word translated "improper" in verse 35, or "shameful" in another translation (ESV). Why would it be "shameful" or "improper" for women to publicly ask questions of men other than their husbands in the assembly of the church?

Simply this: In the culture of that day, women speaking in public was generally frowned upon. Speaking to other women's husbands simply was not done! So, for the sake of those who did not yet understand how the "all are one in Christ" principle played out, Paul tells them to keep silent. Otherwise, visitors would be so offended by the ignoring of proper cultural etiquette that they could not take in what was being said.

Women are free to pray and prophesy within the assembly. But when issues arise that they don't understand, they must refrain from inquiring. Paul does not want any one individual or any group to dominate the gathering (one reason for his instruction in verses 27–31, where he limits how many can speak in tongues and prophesy).

One could reasonably argue that, if this second view is correct, Paul's prohibition in verse 34 on women speaking is no longer applicable, at least in Western society, where there is no shame or impropriety in a woman asking a question in public of another woman's husband. To be perfectly candid, no interpretation is without its problems—reminding us not to be dogmatic on any divisive subject.

The Purpose of Prophecy

Prophetic words edify, exhort, and console (see 1 Corinthians 14:3). When people are suddenly confronted with the reality that God knows their hearts, has heard their prayers, and understands their ways, they are encouraged. I've often met believers who felt as if God had forgotten them. But when a total stranger gives them a prophetic word that could be known only by God Himself, their faith and their spirits rise.

Prophecies bring conviction as secrets of the sinner's heart are exposed (see 1 Corinthians 14:24–25). Paul also envisioned prophecy teaching (see verse 31), and even giving direction for ministry (see Acts 13:1–3).

A young couple was considering whether God was calling them to leave their home and move to Kansas City to train for ministry. They were given a brief but powerful word from a man who had never met them. He said:

> Artie and Jennifer . . . Arthur . . . and is there a Cheryl? You are friends of Sam's from Oklahoma, and you are wondering about whether to move to pursue ministry. Well, pack your bags, because it isn't in Oklahoma.

The significance of these names is that Arthur and Cheryl are Artie's parents! I believe this alerted Artie and Jennifer to the fact that the counsel was accurate. There simply is no way this prophet could have known those names, apart from divine revelation. (This couple had already decided to move to Kansas City, so this was divine confirmation of God's will.)

Finally, prophetic utterances may contain warnings (see Acts 21:4, 10–14) or present opportunities. Prophetic utterances may even identify and impart spiritual gifts (see 1 Timothy 4:14).

How *Not* to Use Prophecy

Let me conclude with a few words about how prophecy is *not* to be used:

1. Prophecy does not establish doctrines or practices that lack explicit biblical support. The Bible is the final and all-sufficient treasury of every doctrine God will ever give. Prophecies don't give new ethical principles. What is right and wrong has been forever settled in the written Word of God.
2. Don't use prophecy to set behavioral standards on secondary issues. Be wary of those who claim it is "God's will"

that Christians engage (or don't engage) in any activities not explicitly advocated or prohibited in Scripture.

3. Never use prophecy to disclose negative or critical information in public. Remember that according to 1 Corinthians 14:3, prophecy is designed to encourage, edify, and console believers. It is not meant to humiliate or embarrass them. Whatever revelation you get is first and foremost for prayer. After you have prayed, God will show you the time and way to speak. All revelation is a call to prayer!

4. Prophets do not have the oversight authority in the Church. Listen to them, seek their counsel and insight. But remember that church leadership is the responsibility of the elders. The New Testament doesn't say, "Be subject to the prophets," but rather, "Be subject to your elders" (1 Peter 5:5; see also Hebrews 13:17). Paul went from city to city to ordain or appoint elders—not prophets (see Acts 14:23; 20:17; 1 Timothy 5:17; 1 Peter 5:2; Titus 1:5). It's good that some elders and pastors are prophetically gifted, but that does not qualify them for office. Elders are to be "able to teach" (1 Timothy 3:2), not to prophesy.

5. Be cautious about depending on prophetic words for making routine decisions in life. In certain situations, guidance from a prophetic word is appropriate, as with the decision confirmed to the young couple above. Even the apostle Paul altered his plans based on prophetic revelation (see Acts 16; Galatians 2:1–2). Paul wrote in 1 Corinthians 16:4, "And if it is appropriate for me to go also, they will go with me." Here, Paul made his decision based on an evaluation of what was "appropriate" or advisable, in view of the circumstances and what he felt would please God. Prophetic insight could have played a role, but Paul also appealed to "knowledge," "discernment," and "spiritual wisdom and

understanding" (Philippians 1:9–10; Colossians 1:9) in the decision-making process. Revelation from the Lord can be important, but God does not want us to be paralyzed in its absence.

6. Never give in to pressure to prophesy, unless you have a divine revelation. Prophetically gifted people sometimes are pressured to perform on demand: "I need a word from God, and I need it now." But *never speak when God is silent.* Severe warnings of judgment are reserved for those who claim to speak for God, but don't (see Ezekiel 13:1–9; Jeremiah 23:25–32).

The Gift of Distinguishing of Spirits

This spiritual gift may be the ability to pass discerning judgment on prophetic utterances, thereby standing in relation to the gift of prophecy the way interpretation relates to the gift of tongues. However, the "others" passing judgment on a prophetic word in 1 Corinthians 14:29 are probably all other believers, not just a select few with a special gift (see more on this in chapter 7).

I'm inclined to believe, however, that this gift of distinguishing spirits is the ability to distinguish between works of the Holy Spirit and works of *another* spirit (demonic), or perhaps even the human spirit. The Holy Spirit does not produce all miracles or supernatural displays. Although all Christians are responsible to "test the spirits to see whether they are from God" (1 John 4:1), Paul has in mind here a gifted ability intuitive in nature. Given the contextual flow in 1 John, all believers should test the spirits by evaluating their messages. First off, do they confess that "Jesus Christ has come in the flesh" (verse 2)? This requires no special gifting. But the spiritual gift of distinguishing of spirits seems to be a supernaturally enabled sense or feeling about the nature and source of the spirit.

Here are some possible instances of this gift's operation:

Acts 16:16–18, where Paul discerned that the power of a slave girl was in fact a demonic spirit.

Acts 13:8–11, where Paul discerned that Elymas was demonically energized in his opposition to the Gospel.

Acts 14:8–10, where again Paul discerned ("saw") that a man had faith to be healed.

A believer may discern whether a problem in someone's life is demonic, or is a consequence of other emotional and psychological factors, or is perhaps a combination of both. People with this gift are often able to detect the presence of demonic spirits in specific locations. In Acts 8:20–24, Peter said he could see (not physically, but he saw or sensed) that Simon Magus was filled with bitterness and iniquity.

Prophecy is certainly a precious gift of God to His people. But that does not mean it is beyond being abused. Perhaps the greatest disservice we show to those who prophesy is failing to evaluate what they say in the light of Scripture. I want to address this very point in the next chapter.

SEVEN

Who Said God Said?

n prophetic ministry today, hearing God's voice with greater clarity isn't the main need. As important as that is, the most urgent need is for the Church to be theologically literate and familiar with the Bible, so that it can effectively judge and evaluate both the source and meaning of dreams, visions, and subjective impressions.

Those of us who happily embrace the gifts of the Spirit need to realize that some in prophetic ministry have been less than diligent students of the written Word of God. This can lead to an inability to effectively test and analyze what purports to be the *spoken* word of God. Some become so enamored by spontaneous revelatory words that they have neglected the Scriptures.

Without a diligent and disciplined study of God's Word, life-changing prophecy can seem the easy route. True, it is harder to actively immerse oneself in the rigors of biblical study than it is to receive an exciting revelatory word from a prophet. But spoken words must never become an excuse for sloth when it comes to digging deeply into God's written Word for the treasures that will otherwise remain unearthed.

We don't pit the written Word of God against the spoken word of God. After all, in the *written* Word Paul told us not to despise the *spoken* word (see 1 Thessalonians 5:20 and elsewhere). But never forget that the *written* Word judges and tests the *spoken word*.

Why are we slack in our duty to judge prophetic words? Some are so accustomed to hearing God's voice and having others expect them to hear it, or to interpret it for those who claim they have heard it, that they tend not to evaluate. They are only too happy to interpret what they believe is the meaning of a word, but they don't bother to *evaluate its origin* against God's written Word. It's easier to take for granted that what purports to be a prophetic word is wholly from God, and scary to acknowledge that some words aren't genuine.

Also, it may be unpleasant to challenge someone concerning the validity of a word he or she has spoken. After all, we don't want to hurt people's feelings or shut them down so that they aren't open to the possibility that God is speaking. This misguided compassion only aggravates the problem.

Others are so concerned about despising prophetic words and quenching the Holy Spirit that they bend over backward not to judge or evaluate what is said. They may fear that if they misjudge a prophetic word, they might lose the blessing God intended for them. They don't want to appear skeptical of what may be the voice of heaven. This must stop. Let me simply remind you that the apostle Paul was in no way offended or put off by the Bereans, who examined the Scriptures to determine whether what he said was true (see Acts 17:10–11). He commended them! Prophecy is too precious and too important to let this sort of abuse continue any longer.

Some who believe in the gift of prophecy and want to excel in its exercise overreact to the skepticism of those Christians who believe that prophecy died with the apostle John. This overreaction has resulted in an equally dangerous response:

gullibility and an empty-headed acceptance of any so-called word that is uttered. Both responses destroy prophecy's effectiveness in the Church.

The Biblical Mandate

Look at Paul's counsel in 1 Thessalonians 5:19–22. This entire passage is specifically describing the responsibility of the entire Church to judge prophetic utterances:

- "Do not quench the Spirit" (verse 19).
- "Do not despise prophecies" (verse 20 ESV).
- "But examine everything" carefully (verse 21).
- "Hold firmly to that which is good" (verse 21).
- "Abstain from every form of evil" (verse 22).

Observe the parallel between verses 19 and 20. Paul's exhortation in verse 19 not to quench the Spirit refers to our response to prophecy in verse 20. It may well have application to the exercise of other spiritual gifts in the Church, but its first and primary reference is to the gift of prophecy. The Spirit's activity of imparting revelation is compared to a fire that we must not douse with skepticism, religiosity, or fear.

Perhaps most important is the "but" with which verse 21 opens. Paul is setting up a contrast. Rather than quench the Holy Spirit by despising prophetic utterances, we are to *examine everything*. "Everything" (or "all things") in verse 21 refers to the prophetic utterances in verse 20. This leads to the conclusion that the "good" to which we are to hold firmly (verse 21), and the "evil" from which we are to abstain (verse 22) also refer to prophetic utterances (verse 20).

Many think that verses 21–22 are a general exhortation to help us respond to good and evil in the world. Yet when looked at in the light of the overall context, we see that the "good" is prophetic utterances that truly come from God and encourage, edify, and console, but that the "evil" refers to what alleges to be God's revelation but in fact is not, having been shown to be inconsistent with Scripture.

The fact that Paul even felt compelled to *write* this is remarkably instructive! For one thing, it tells us that not everyone in the early Church was completely happy about the gift of prophecy. Some were taking steps to suppress its exercise. This is especially remarkable because it was happening in the Church at Thessalonica, one of the most godly and mature early congregations (see 1 Thessalonians 1:1–10).

Why were some in Thessalonica "despising" (ESV) or "treating with contempt" (NIV) prophetic words, as 1 Thessalonians 5:20 warned them not to do? Probably for the same reason that people do so today! Undoubtedly, the prophetic gift had been abused in Thessalonica, prompting some to call for its elimination. Some may have abused the gift by using it to control other people's lives, or to increase their own sphere of influence and power in the Church.

People often mistakenly assume that a prophecy is an infallible guarantee, when a prophecy more often is an invitation or exhortation. We know that the Thessalonians were skittish about alleged prophetic words, as the scenario described in 2 Thessalonians 2:1–2 makes clear.

But don't miss what Paul was saying: It doesn't matter how badly people may have abused this gift. It is a sin to despise prophecy. This is a divine command. Don't treat prophecy with contempt; don't treat it as if it were unimportant; don't trivialize it. Don't throw the treasure of what is true out with the trash of what has been proven false!

This exhortation also means that if you do despise prophecy, if you seek to exclude it from your church life, if you flippantly disregard it, you have "quenched the Holy Spirit." You have put

72

out His fire! That is incredibly revealing about how the Holy Spirit ministers through us. He will rarely, if ever, force Himself in a manifestation of a gift or any other expression. The Spirit willingly subjects Himself to the will and timing of the believer (see 1 Corinthians 14:32). The Holy Spirit does not act upon or through us as if we were puppets. The sovereign Spirit happily subjects Himself to our decision concerning when and how we deliver prophetic words. (Another good reason to pray and consult Him for the best way and timing!) Not only that, but you also can put out the Spirit's fire burning in someone else's heart. That's dangerous ground!

So, what's the alternative to not quenching the Holy Spirit when He speaks prophetically through someone? It isn't "anything goes." Rather, we are to test, judge, or examine every word. Paul didn't correct abuse by commanding *disuse* (as with many noncharismatics). We are not to gullibly believe every word that is spoken, nor are we to cynically reject all words. Paul's remedy for sinful despising was *biblically informed discernment*. When prophecies are given, we are to test, examine, evaluate, assess, weigh, and judge these "utterances" (NASB1995). Paul commands us to (1) examine everything, (2) hold fast to that which is good, and (3) abstain from every form of evil. Let's look at practical ways to do these things.

Examining everything carefully

Paul first commanded the believers to "examine everything." By "everything," Paul meant "all prophetic utterances." But how do we do this?

The early Church was to evaluate prophecies in the light of the apostolic traditions bequeathed them by Paul. In 2 Thessalonians 2:15, the reference to what they were "taught . . . by word of mouth" alludes to the oral instruction and preaching of Paul during his stay in Thessalonica. The "letter" Paul mentioned likely refers to either to 1 or 2 Thessalonians.

For us, all prophetic words must conform to Scripture. In the wilderness, Jesus tested Satan's words against Scripture and exposed how the enemy was misapplying it (see Matthew 4:1–11).

According to 1 Corinthians 14:3, we must always ask this question of a prophecy: Does a word build up and strengthen, or does it tear down and create disunity, fear, doubt, or self-contempt? If the word is predictive, find out if the event came to pass as prophesied.

We must also apply the test of love (see 1 Corinthians 13), by which all charismatic gifts are to be measured. Paul didn't care much for any gift of the Spirit if it violated love.

The test of community is also important. Wisdom demands that we always present a prophetic word to others who are experienced evaluators.

Finally, there is the test of personal experience. When Paul was given a word about the danger that awaited him in Jerusalem (see Acts 21:3–4, 10–14), he evaluated it and then responded in light of what God had already shown him (Acts 20:22–23). In effect, Paul said, "Yes, we all got the same revelation. We agree on the interpretation—suffering awaits me in Jerusalem. But we differ on its application. I'm still going!"

Hold fast to the good

Paul's second exhortation is to "hold firmly to that which is good." Once you have determined that a word is good, is biblical, and meets all other criteria, it most probably is from God—so believe, obey, and preserve it.

Abstain from every form of evil

Paul's third exhortation was to "abstain from every form of evil." The word "abstain" (or avoid) is also found in 1 Thessalonians 4:3 ("abstain from sexual immorality") and 1 Timothy 4:3 ("[abstain] from foods"). The word translated "form" (or kind) is used only here in Paul's writings. Hence, we are to shun every kind of prophetic utterance that doesn't conform to Scripture, that doesn't build up, encourage, and console. *That kind of word is an evil word.*

Some Concluding Thoughts

1. Prophets can speak both good and evil words. But evil comes in various shades; it may mean the word isn't effective or fruitful. Or evil may mean "contrary to Scripture." It doesn't necessarily mean "hateful, mean, wicked, or harmful." It simply fails to accomplish what true prophetic words are designed by God to accomplish.

2. We must not assume that every idea or image or word that pops into our heads (or the head of a recognized prophet) is a revelation from God. Remember, all revelations are first a matter for prayer. We can always pray into that situation, for that person, inviting God to confirm His word and direct us in its delivery.

3. There is a vast difference between prophesying falsely and being a false prophet. All of us have probably spoken words we *thought* were from God that, in fact, were not. But that doesn't make us false prophets. It just makes us human! False prophets are indeed spoken of in the New Testament, but they were not believers who made errors. False prophets were unbelieving enemies of the Gospel (see Matthew 7:15–23; 24:10–11, 24; 2 Peter 2:1–3; 1 John 4:1–6).

4. In 1 Corinthians 14:29, Paul wrote, "Have two or three prophets speak, and have *the others* pass judgment" (emphasis added). Does Paul's statement imply that more speakers would violate God's Word? If so, his point would be to limit the number to three, lest those with this gift dominate the meeting. There is similar instruction in

75

verse 27 concerning those who speak in tongues. On the other hand, verses 24 and 31 seem to suggest that many might prophesy in a meeting. In that case, there should be no more than three at a time before the others weigh carefully what is said. Verse 29 may be designed to restrict how many speak in sequence, not the total number of prophecies given in a service.

5. The "others" who are to pass judgment are probably the other believers present. The instruction in 1 Thessalonians 5:20–21 is directed to the entire Church, not a special group. This judgment isn't the determination of whether an utterance is of the devil, but whether it's compatible with what the Spirit has already said (in Scripture, in the apostolic tradition, etc.). If New Testament congregational prophecy is occasionally a mixture of divine revelation and human interpretation and application (see Acts 21:4–6; 10–14, 27–35), it's essential that the Church evaluate and analyze what is said, accepting only what is right (see again 1 Thessalonians 5:19–22, and also 1 John 4:1–6). Paul's command points to the assumption that some of what the prophets say could be erroneous or misleading.

The takeaway from this chapter is simple: When a prophetic word is delivered to you, open your Bible. Assess what was said. To do so doesn't show unbelief or suspicion of the person who spoke the word. It's your obligation. As each one determines not to be a skeptic who puts out the Spirit's fire, so determine also not to be a fool who believes without examination.

It is a beautiful thing that God should find it important and helpful to reveal Himself to His children in personal and intimate ways. This bears witness to the fact that the sufficiency of the Bible doesn't mean that we no longer need to hear from our heavenly Father. Scripture never claims to supply us with all possible information necessary to make every conceivable decision. Scripture may tell us to preach the Gospel to all people, but it doesn't tell a new missionary that God wants her in Albania, not Australia. The potential for God to speak beyond Scripture, whether for guidance, exhortation, encouragement, or conviction of sin, does not threaten the sufficiency of Scripture.

EIGHT

What Is the Gift of Tongues?

thank God, I speak in tongues more than you all."

These sound like the words of a flamboyant charismatic on television—but they are the words of Paul of Tarsus, apostle of Jesus Christ (1 Corinthians 14:18). Evidently, Paul's spiritual life regularly featured praying, singing, and praising in tongues, and he was not embarrassed to say so. Indeed, he was profoundly grateful to God!

If nothing else, this ought to make us pause before we too quickly dismiss tongues as the habit of ill-informed fanatics. The gift of tongues is simply the Spirit-energized ability to pray, worship, give thanks, or speak in a language other than your own or one you might have learned in school.

The gift of tongues has been a divisive and controversial issue. In a world of heated church squabbles, nothing compares to the hostility provoked over contemporary tongues-speech!

I was raised in a tradition that viewed speaking in tongues as something ignorant and undignified that people did, probably on the verge of a seizure—or so I was told. People who hoped to make their mark in the world wouldn't mutter gibberish or associate with those who did. Or so I was told.

For many years, I mocked those who claimed to experience this phenomenon. But don't let that harden you against the possibility that this might well be a gift of God. We must never forget that the gift of tongues was *God's idea*, not man's. He gave this gift to the Church no less than the gifts of teaching, mercy, exhortation, and evangelism. Let's resolve from the outset not to spurn or ridicule something precious in *God's* sight, graciously bestowed by a loving heavenly Father who gives only good gifts to His children. Let's also keep the perspective that tongues are neither God's greatest gift to His most highly favored children, nor the devil's most sinister tool of deceit.

Tongues are like any other gift of the Spirit—not a sign of God's special love or of heightened maturity in Christ. Not a sign of superior zeal. Not a sign that one has more of the Holy Spirit. Tongues are merely one gift among many that Paul calls the "manifestation of the Spirit" given to believers for the common good of the Church (1 Corinthians 12:7).

Contrary to the opinions of many who don't have of the gift of tongues, those who have it testify that it has enhanced and deepened their relationship with the Lord Jesus—precisely what prayer and praise are supposed to do! This gift of the Spirit has a terrible public image. I encourage you to search the Scriptures, seek the face of God, and continue reading as I attempt to provide a biblical foundation for understanding and exercising this gift.

Read what follows with your Bible open. If what I say doesn't measure up to the written Word of God, dump it. Experience is good only as it reflects the teaching of Scripture. Often, people who believe in the gifts of the Holy Spirit are considered too lazy to think, or afraid that the Bible contradicts their experience. But let's never be afraid of the Bible!

Were Tongues Evangelistic?

Some cessationists argue that tongues were an evangelistic sign-gift for unbelieving Jews. But there is *no* evidence that tongues-speech was designed to evangelize unbelievers. That isn't to say God couldn't use it to save souls, but that's not its primary purpose.

When people spoke in tongues, they declared "the mighty deeds of God" (Acts 2:11; see also Acts 10:46; 19:17). The people heard *worship*. Peter's preaching was what brought salvation. We see that the primary purpose of tongues-speech is to address God, whether in praise or prayer (see 1 Corinthians 14:2, 14). And when the household of Cornelius spoke in tongues, Peter concluded that they were saved and thus eligible to be baptized in water, just like the Jews who accepted Jesus (see Acts 10:47).

Only in Acts 2 are tongues explicitly said to be human languages not previously learned by those speaking them. Nowhere in Acts did speaking in tongues function as an evangelistic tool. In the three explicit references to tongues in Acts, only once are unbelievers present (in Acts 2). Those who argue that tongues were primarily an evangelistic sign-gift for unbelieving Jews miss the fact that only believers were present at two of these three occurrences of tongues.

Tongues-Speech in 1 Corinthians

Many passages in Paul's letters seem to refer to tongues, but let's focus on several principles from 1 Corinthians 12–14.

Before turning there, however, I need to make one comment. Some point out that tongues-speech is not explicitly mentioned in a New Testament epistle, except in 1 Corinthians (unless Ephesians 6:18 and Romans 8:26–27 refer to tongues). So they conclude that the gift of tongues was either infrequently exercised or "on its way out," so to speak. But this is an argument from silence. If we consistently applied that argument to Scripture, we would also have to say that the Lord's Supper is explicitly mentioned only in 1 Corinthians. Was it then infrequently observed or becoming obsolete? You see the point!

Furthermore, the silence of other New Testament epistles can just as easily be explained by the fact that, unlike in Corinth, tongues were not a problem in the other churches to whom Paul wrote. There was no need for him to address it.

It's unfortunate that the image many have of speaking in tongues is shaped by their familiarity with one somewhat negative statement Paul made in 1 Corinthians 13:1: "If I speak with the tongues of mankind and of angels, but do not have love, I have become a noisy gong or a clanging cymbal." But let's not forget that Paul is dealing with the *abuse* of this spiritual gift in Corinth. If Paul were writing to a church in which the gift of tongues was properly employed, perhaps his words would have been, "If I speak with the tongues of mankind and of angels and do so with love, the sound is like a symphony that pleases the ear."

The problem in Corinth was *not* that the believers spoke in tongues, but that some who did so thought themselves spiritually superior to those who didn't. To make matters worse, they were using the gift in the public gathering of the church *without accompanying interpretation*. Paul addressed the first problem in 1 Corinthians 12–13, and the second in chapter 14.

The Nature of Tongues

Pauls' main concern in 1 Corinthians 14 was edifying believers in the church (see verses 3–6, 12, 17, 19, 26). Other people can be built up in their faith only if they understand what is being said—the reason he insisted that tongues in the assembly must be interpreted.

Don't misunderstand Paul's contrasts: Prophecy is superior to uninterpreted tongues only because it is intelligible and edifies others. When tongues are interpreted, they become a functional equivalent of prophecy (see 1 Corinthians 14:5). Uninterpreted tongues can't edify others; that's the only reason they are regarded as inferior to prophecy. Interpreted tongues *do edify*, so don't forbid them (see verse 39).

Paul was not suggesting that prophecy is the most important gift or that the gift of tongues is the least important. He was only saying that uninterpreted tongues are less valuable than prophecy in the gathered assembly. How tongues or prophecy might compare with apostleship or teaching or any other gift wasn't Paul's point.

Paul's command in 1 Corinthians 12:31 and in 1 Corinthians 14:1 and 39, as well as his statement in 14:12, all indicate that we are to desire and seek spiritual gifts! Far from being a sign of immaturity or an illegal hankering after sensational phenomena (as some contend), seeking spiritual gifts is a moral and biblical obligation for all Christians.

Paul's statement in 1 Corinthians 14:2 is crucial for understanding tongues:

1. Tongues-speech is directed to God. Tongues are fundamentally worship and intercession. Even when interpreted in a public gathering, tongues-speech is God oriented.
2. No one in the Church understands tongues when it is uninterpreted. This is the reason for the relative "inferiority" of tongues to prophecy.
3. Paul said that "in" or "by" his spirit (and the Holy Spirit?), he speaks mysteries. But whose spirit did Paul have in mind? In 1 Corinthians 12:7–11, we are told that "gifts" are manifestations of the Holy Spirit. Perhaps Paul meant that the Holy Spirit exercises the gift through the human spirit.

83

4. What is meant by *mysteries*? Possibly, truths relating to our salvation that were not previously revealed, but now have been made known. But more likely, Paul was referring to anything that lies outside the understanding of both the speaker and the hearer. In other words, a speaker in tongues speaks mysteries in the sense that no one understands. Tongues-speech, when uninterpreted, is simply a mystery to everyone.

Prophecy, on the other hand, does what uninterpreted tongues cannot do. It is preferred in the public gathering of the Church for that reason. Prophecy edifies and exhorts and consoles (see 1 Corinthians 14:3).

Self-Edification

Some say Paul was rebuking anyone who desires to be edified by tongues as selfish. But edifying oneself is not a bad thing. Paul says it simply isn't the point of a public meeting. We study the Bible, pray, and listen to sermons to edify ourselves. And Jude 20 *commands* us to edify ourselves by praying in the Spirit!

Every gift of the Spirit in some way edifies its user. This is only a problem when self-edification is one's selfish focus. If your spiritual gift increases your maturity, expands your understanding, and intensifies your zeal, it's better for the Body of Christ!

Also, if self-edification from tongues-speech were wrong, Paul would not have encouraged its use in the first part of 1 Corinthians 14:5. And clearly, uninterpreted tongues were what Paul contrasted with prophecy, insisting that prophecy is better suited to edify others (unless, of course, the tongues-speech is interpreted, as the second part of verse 5 mentions).

Is tongues-speech an ecstatic experience? Many define *ecstatic* as a mental or emotional state in which the person is oblivious and seems to lose self-control, perhaps lapsing into a condition in which rational thinking is lost.

First, remember that the New Testament never uses the term *ecstasy* to describe speaking in tongues. It is found in some English translations, but it is not in the Greek. There is no indication in the Bible that people who speak in tongues lose self-control or become unaware of their surroundings. In fact, Paul insists that the one who is speaking in tongues can start and stop at will (see 1 Corinthians 14:15–19; 27–28; 40; compare to 14:32). There is a vast difference between an experience being *ecstatic* and being *emotional*. Tongues can be an emotionally exhilarating experience, bringing peace and joy, but that does not mean they are ecstatic.

Can Everyone Speak in Tongues?

Paul nowhere downplayed or despised the gift of tongues. He wished all believers spoke in tongues (see 1 Corinthians 14:5). He applauded the capacity of tongues to edify the believer (see verse 4). He thanked God for tongues in his own prayer life, and he explicitly said not to forbid the exercise of this gift (see verses 18–19, 39).

But we're still left with the most controversial issue relating to tongues-speech: Does Paul's statement in 1 Corinthians 14:5 mean that *all* Christians should or will speak in tongues? Those who say no argue this way:

1. In 1 Corinthians 7:7, Paul uses language identical to what is found in 14:5: "I wish that all men were even as I myself am" (referring to his celibacy). No one will argue that Paul intended for all Christians to be celibate, as he was. Surely, then, we should not expect all to speak in tongues either.
2. According to 1 Corinthians 12:7–11, tongues, like the other gifts mentioned, are bestowed to individuals *as the*

Holy Spirit wills. They are gifts, not entitlements! If Paul meant that all were to experience this gift, why did he employ the terminology of "to one is given . . . and to another . . . and to another . . ."?

3. In 1 Corinthians 12:30, Paul quite explicitly stated that "all do not speak with tongues," any more than all are apostles, or all are teachers, or all have gifts of healings, and so on (see verses 28–30).

Some may ask, "Why would God withhold from any of His children a gift that enables them to pray and to praise Him so effectively, a gift that also functions to edify them in their faith?" And does not 1 Corinthians 14:23 at least imply that the potential exists for all to speak in tongues?

Some people believe the answer lies in looking at the setting in which tongues are exercised. Perhaps 1 Corinthians 12:7–11 and 28–30 refer to the gift in public ministry, whereas 1 Corinthians 14 is describing the gift in private devotion. In 1 Corinthians 12:28, Paul specifically said he was describing what happens "in the church" or in the assembly (compare with 1 Corinthians 11:18; 14:19, 23, 28, 33, 35). Not everyone is gifted by the Spirit to speak in tongues during the corporate gathering of a church. But the potential does exist for every believer to pray in tongues in private. These are not two different gifts, but two different *contexts* in which the gift might be employed. A person who ministers to an entire church in tongues is someone who already uses tongues in his or her prayer life.

Jack Hayford suggests that the *gift* of tongues is:

(1) limited in distribution (1 Cor. 12:11, 30), and
(2) its public exercise is to be closely governed (1 Cor. 14:27–28);

(3) while the *grace* of tongues is so broadly available that Paul wished that all enjoyed its blessing (1 Cor. 14:5a), which includes

(4) distinctive communication with God (1 Cor. 14:2);

(5) edifying of the believer's private life (1 Cor. 14:4);

(6) worship and thanksgiving with beauty and propriety (see 1 Cor. 14:15–17).[1]

The difference between these operations of the Holy Spirit is that not every Christian might expect to exercise the public gift, while any Christian may expect and welcome the *private grace* of spiritual language in his or her personal time of fellowship with God, praiseful worship before God, and intercessory prayer to God (see 1 Corinthians 14:2, 15–17; Romans 8:26–27).

Paul's point at the end of 1 Corinthians 12 is that not every believer will contribute to the Body in precisely the same way. Not everyone will minister a prophetic word, not everyone will teach, and so on. But whether everyone might pray privately in tongues is not in Paul's purview until 1 Corinthians 14.

Consider what Paul said about prophecy: "All are not prophets, are they?" (1 Corinthians 12:29). No, of course not. But Paul is quick to say that the potential exists for all to prophesy (see 1 Corinthians 14:1, 31). Why could not the same be true for tongues? Couldn't Paul have been saying that although all do not speak in tongues in corporate public ministry, all may speak in tongues as an expression of private praise and prayer? Just as Paul's rhetorical question in 1 Corinthians 12:29 is not designed to rule out the possibility that anyone may utter a prophetic word, so also his question in verse 30 is not designed to exclude anyone from using tongues in his or her devotional experience.

To be honest, I must confess that it seems unlikely that God would withhold the gift of tongues from one of His children who passionately and sincerely desired it. After all, if you deeply desire this gift, it's probably because the Holy Spirit has stirred your heart to seek for it. And He has stirred your heart to seek for it because it's His will to bestow it. So, if you long for the gift of tongues, persevere in your prayers. My sense is that God will answer you in His time!

Paul's Prayer Life

Paul described his own gift of speaking in tongues this way in 1 Corinthians 14:14: "my spirit prays." This may be a reference to the Holy Spirit, or perhaps to his own human spirit, or even a co-working of the two, which in effect constitutes the essence of a spiritual gift. (Remember, a spiritual gift is the Holy Spirit energizing my spirit to do what otherwise I couldn't do.) Look back at this verse again. When Paul prays in tongues, his mind is "unfruitful" (NIV). By this he means either, "I don't understand what I'm saying," or "Other people don't understand what I'm saying." The first is more likely.

Many insist that if one's mind is unfruitful—not engaged in such a way that the believer's mind is in control—then the experience is useless. The apostle Paul strongly disagreed. Since Paul asserted that his mind was unfruitful when he prayed in tongues, many would expect him to repudiate the use of tongues altogether—but he doesn't!

What benefit can there be in a spiritual experience that one's mind can't comprehend? Look closely at Paul's conclusion. He even introduced his conclusion by asking the question, in view of what has just been said in verse 14, "What is the outcome then?" (verse 15). He was determined to do both! He goes on in verse 15 to say, "I will pray with the spirit" (i.e., I will pray in tongues), and "I will pray with the mind also" (i.e., I will pray in Greek so that others who speak and understand Greek can profit from what I say). Clearly, Paul believed that a spiritual experience beyond the grasp of his mind was deeply profitable. Paul believed that an experience did not have to be cognitive for it to be spiritually beneficial and glorifying to God.

This doesn't dismiss the importance of one's mind. In Romans 12:2, Paul commanded that we experience renewal in our minds. All I'm saying—what I believe Paul is saying—is that praying in tongues is eminently beneficial. It glorifies God even though it is *transrational* (going beyond my mind).

Furthermore, since Paul was determined to pray with the spirit (i.e., pray in uninterpreted tongues), where and when would he do it? Since he ruled out doing it in the public meeting, he must have been referring to his private, devotional prayer life. To "sing in or with the spirit" is to sing in tongues—a sung form of tongues-speech, another practice that seems to have characterized Paul's private prayer.

Paul goes further in 1 Corinthians 14:18–19. Clearly, praying, singing, and praising in tongues characterized Paul's devotional life, and he was grateful to God for this gift. His point in verse 19 is simple: The issue is not whether one speaks in tongues, but what is appropriate in the Church. Paul had prohibited tongues-speech in the public gathering without interpretation. Because the purpose of church meetings is building up believers, Paul rarely spoke in tongues in a public setting.

Now, note well: If Paul spoke in tongues more than anyone else, yet in church he almost never did (preferring there to speak in a way all could understand), where did he speak in tongues? Paul must have exercised his gift in the context of his personal intimacy with God. Remember, this is the man who wrote Romans by the inspiration of God's Spirit, and whose incomparable mind God used to disable theological opponents and take out Athenian philosophers (see Acts 17). Logical, reasonable, highly educated Paul prayed in tongues more than anyone!

Are Tongues a Sign?

According to 1 Corinthians 14:22, the answer is yes, tongues are a sign. But let's first make sense of the scenario Paul envisions. According to verse 23 (ESV), Paul envisions a public assembly: "[when] the whole church comes together." The purpose of such a gathering is not only to praise and pray, but also to instruct, encourage, and build up the Body. Everything that happens must be intelligible.

The problem in Corinth was that people were speaking in uninterpreted tongues simultaneously—no one understood, so no one was instructed. They were speaking in genuine tongues, praying and giving thanks, but to no one's benefit other than their own and God's.

So, Paul says that when you come together, if anyone speaks in a tongue, be sure there is an interpretation (1 Corinthians 14:26–27). Otherwise the tongue speaker should be quiet (verse 28). Prophecy, on the other hand, is a sign of God's presence with believers (see verse 22), so Paul encourages its use when *unbelievers* are present so that they may see, hear, and come to faith in Jesus (see verses 24–25). Uninterpreted tongues-speech is not to be done in church. It's that simple!

Tongues in the Church

Some Corinthian believers exhibited two errors:

1. They overemphasized tongues' importance, thinking that those who exercised this gift must be more favored of God. Immaturity led them to conclude that tongues-speech was evidence of superior spirituality.
2. They were employing (indeed, flaunting) their tongues-speech in the public assembly without interpretation. Paul's

response was not to ban the gift of tongues, but to correct them. Abuse does not nullify the reality of a divine gift. He did not reject, but corrected.

Briefly, the apostle's counsel was this in 1 Corinthians 14:26–40: Take steps to prevent a simultaneous cacophony of tongues-speech. Allow only two, or at most three, to speak during a service. Why? So that the meeting does not become disorderly or unwieldy, and so that those with the gift of tongues don't assume a more prominent place in the Body. The tongues speaker should never think that the gift is beyond control. The Holy Spirit does not compel or overwhelm.

If the two or three had already spoken, Paul expected the others to keep quiet (clearly, they had control over their gift). Paul would not accept the excuse, "But I just couldn't help myself. The presence and power and impulse of the Holy Spirit were just too much for me to contain. I would have been quenching the Spirit's work had I kept silent!" No. The Holy Spirit never moves or prompts someone to violate what He has previously said in Scripture.

I've already shown in 1 Corinthians 14:14–19 that praying in tongues was a staple experience in Paul's devotional life. This is confirmed by verse 28, where he instructed what should be done in the absence of an interpreter: "Have him [the tongues speaker] speak to himself and to God." Where? Given the explicit prohibition of uninterpreted tongues-speech "in the church," it seems likely that Paul had in mind prayer in tongues in private.

Furthermore, why would Paul emphasize in 1 Corinthians 14 all working together for mutual edification, and then say that some (perhaps many) focus their spiritual energy inwardly (praying in tongues) while someone else is speaking outwardly? Why try to edify the very people who aren't even paying attention?

Corporate Singing in the Spirit

A question I'm often asked is whether it is biblically permissible to sing in uninterpreted tongues in a corporate setting. Many would immediately say no and point to Paul's statement in 1 Corinthians 14:28: "But if there is no interpreter, he [the tongues speaker] is to keep silent in church; and have him speak to himself and to God [presumably in private]."

Of one thing, I'm sure: If the corporate gathering is an official church service, the point of which is to edify the Body (see 1 Corinthians 14:26), then uninterpreted tongues are not permissible. This is what accounts for Paul's demand for silence in verse 28.

But what if the gathering is one at which only believers are in attendance? What if the purpose is praise and intercession? In such a meeting, uninterpreted tongues are no obstacle to achieving the purpose for which people have congregated. Therefore, corporate singing in the Spirit would not violate Paul's counsel.

My Experience with Tongues

My first encounter with the gifts of the Spirit came when I was nineteen years old, serving with Campus Crusade for Christ on an evangelistic project. A friend invited me to a meeting at which Harald Bredesen, an early leader of the charismatic movement, spoke. What Bredesen said that night sparked my desire for this gift of tongues. I began to pray earnestly to God that, if the gift were real, and in accordance with His will, He might give it to me. For several weeks, I spent each night in a secluded place, pleading with God for His will for me concerning this gift.

One night, quite without warning, my prayer in English was interrupted by words of another sound and form. I distinctly remember thinking to myself, *Sam, what are you saying? Are you speaking in tongues?* I was both frightened and exhilarated. The experience lasted only a couple of minutes, but I felt closer to God than ever before.

Filled with excitement, I called a friend. When I later sat down in his car, I said, "You'll never guess what happened tonight!"

"You spoke in tongues, didn't you?" he asked, deadpan.

"Yes! It was great! But I don't understand what it means."

My friend didn't want to stifle me, but his next words affected me for years to come: "Sam, you realize, don't you, that if people find out about this, you'll likely be excluded from any leadership position on campus? And I hate to say it, but a lot of people will think you're demonized."

I was crushed. I remember feebly and fearfully trying to speak in tongues the next night, but nothing happened. Not wanting to forfeit my position in campus ministry, I concluded that it must have been something other than the Holy Spirit. I explained it away as something I'd be better off not mentioning to anyone else. I never spoke in tongues again for twenty years!

Twenty years later, I was with Jack Deere at a conference. I shared my story with him. He reminded me of something the apostle Paul said to young Timothy: "For this reason I remind you to kindle afresh the gift of God which is in you through the laying on of my hands" (2 Timothy 1:6). Jack then laid hands on me and asked the Lord to kindle this gift afresh in me that He had bestowed so long ago.

This verse in 2 Timothy is important. As I indicated earlier, it tells us that one may receive a spiritual gift—and yet neglect it. Paul's imagery of a flame that needs to be fanned is helpful. If it is not nurtured and used in the way God intended, the once brightly burning flame can become a smoldering ember. Study, pray, seek God's face, put it into practice; do what you need to do to stoke the fire until that gift returns.

I applied Paul's advice to Timothy to myself: Every day, if only for a few minutes, I prayed that God would renew what

He had given, but I had quenched. I prayed that, if it was His will, I would once more be able to pray in the Spirit, to speak that heavenly language that would praise and thank and bless Him (see 1 Corinthians 14:2, 16–17). In faith, I began simply to speak aloud syllables and words God brought to mind. He renewed His precious gift!

Praying in the Spirit is by no means the most important gift. Neither is it a sign of a spirituality or maturity greater than that of those who do not have it. But if the apostle Paul can say, "I thank God, I speak in tongues more than you all," who am I to despise this blessed gift of God?

NINE

Tongues and Interpretation in the Church

A re tongues human languages? I have spoken to many who tell of undeniable instances, often on the mission field, in which a believer spoke in a genuine human language without any previous exposure to it or study of it. I am inclined to believe them. But were all tongues in the New Testament human languages?

Acts 2 is the only text in the New Testament where tongues-speech is reported in foreign languages not previously known by the speaker. This is an important text, yet there is no reason to think that Acts 2, rather than, say, 1 Corinthians 14, is the standard by which all occurrences of tongues-speech must be judged. To begin with, if tongues-speech is *always* in a foreign language intended as a sign for unbelievers, why are the tongues in Acts 10 and Acts 19 spoken in the presence of only believers? Note also that Paul describes various kinds of tongues in 1 Corinthians

12:10. His words suggest differing categories of tongues-speech, perhaps human languages and heavenly languages.

Paul asserted that whoever speaks in a tongue "does not speak to people, but to God" (1 Corinthians 14:2). But if tongues are always human languages, Paul is mistaken, for "speaking to people" is precisely what a human language does! If tongues-speech is always a human language, how could Paul say that "no one understands" in the same verse? If tongues are human languages, *many* could potentially understand, as they did on the day of Pentecost (see Acts 2:8–11), and then the gift of interpretation would not be necessary. God's Spirit would not be required; a person with translation skills could interpret tongues-speech.

Some say 1 Corinthians 14:10–11 refers to earthly foreign languages, and that this proves that all tongues-speech is also human language. But the point is that tongues *function like* foreign languages, not that tongues *are* foreign languages. Paul's point is that the hearer cannot understand uninterpreted tongues any more than he can understand a foreign language. If tongues were a foreign language, there would be no need for the analogy.

Also, Paul's statement in 1 Corinthians 14:18 that he "speak[s] in tongues more than you all" is evidence that tongues are not foreign languages. Finally, if tongues-speech is always human language, Paul's statement in 1 Corinthians 14:23 wouldn't necessarily hold true that "if the whole church gathers together and all the people speak in tongues, and outsiders or unbelievers enter, will they not say that you are insane?" Any unbeliever who would know the language being spoken would more likely conclude that the person speaking was highly educated, not mad.

What Is the Purpose of Tongues-Speech?

Let's look carefully at what Paul says in 1 Corinthians 12–14 to discern several reasons God bestowed this gift.

Speaking in tongues is primarily a form of prayer, communicating with God in praise, petition, and intercession (see again 1 Corinthians 14:2). If Ephesians 6:18 has tongues in view, then tongues are also a weapon in our arsenal for spiritual warfare. If tongues are prayer, one might expect God to sovereignly use this gift in any number of ways for His purposes.

"The one who speaks in a tongue edifies himself" (1 Corinthians 14:4), and self-edification is a command: "But you, beloved, building yourselves up on your most holy faith, praying in the Holy Spirit" (Jude 20).

Speaking in tongues is a form of blessing God's Person and works (see 1 Corinthians 14:16). Hence, tongues-speech is a form of praise (especially "singing in the Spirit"), which can energize our human abilities to praise in a way we otherwise cannot.

Speaking in tongues helps us in our weakness and ignorance in praying for ourselves and others (see Romans 8:26–27). We can pray in tongues when our minds wander and we struggle to focus, when we are physically tired, or when people distract us or there is noise around us.

When we've run out of things to pray for, we can pray in the Spirit. When we don't know someone's pain or problem, or when we feel inadequate to intercede for a person, we may pray in tongues, confident that the Holy Spirit will articulate through us to the Father precisely that person's most urgent needs. Thus, tongues forever eliminate the excuse "I don't know what to say."

Why Does Tongues-Speech Seem Rapid?

People often have heard others pray in tongues with great rapidity, or they themselves have experienced this phenomenon. The Scriptures don't address the issue, so I can't be dogmatic.

Yet perhaps this rapidity is because *the Holy Spirit is praying* through us, and thus prayer in tongues is done at a higher level of spiritual energy (see Acts 2:4; 1 Corinthians 14:14–15).

Also, since the Holy Spirit is articulating our prayers, there is no hesitation over which words to speak, and no stammering in our speech. Fear or self-consciousness is gone, and one need never pause to think of something to say.

Why Are People So Afraid of Tongues?

Here are some reasons that people are so afraid of tongues:

1. Christians who were raised and nurtured in Bible-based churches are fearful of anything artificial in Christian experience. Often, this caution is born of a fear that paralyzes faith and a willingness to risk. After first speaking in what they hope is tongues, the slightest doubt of its authenticity prompts these believers never to try again. But in being passionate for what is genuine, we must not let fear of artificiality control our lives.

2. After first speaking in tongues, people conclude that it didn't feel sufficiently *supernatural*. It didn't seem significantly different from what it takes to pray in English. So, either it wasn't real or it isn't worth the effort. The initial experience with tongues often seems like incoherent gibberish. "How could something so trite and repetitious be of any spiritual value?" people ask. This can lead to their abandoning the practice altogether.

3. Many fear "sounding silly" or appearing foolish before people whose respect matters to them. This often paralyzes their passion for this spiritual gift. Fear of rejection by those people (and loss of ministry, recognition, etc.) can drive this.

Advice for Those Who Don't Speak in Tongues

Let me conclude our discussion of tongues-speech with seven comments designed especially for those who do not have this gift, but perhaps feel a tug in their hearts to ask for it.

Don't be afraid.

Many people have been frightened off with warnings of a counterfeit experience or demonic influence. Yet Paul never gave any warning about counterfeit tongues. Recently converted men and women from pagan and demonic backgrounds filled the church at Corinth. To these people, Paul said, "I wish that you all spoke in tongues" (1 Corinthians 14:5). Nowhere does Paul say or suggest, "I want you all to be afraid of tongues." Paul's counsel is grounded in what Jesus said:

> Now which one of you fathers will his son ask for a fish, and instead of a fish, he will give him a snake? Or he will even ask for an egg, and his father will give him a scorpion? So if you, despite being evil, know how to give good gifts to your children, how much more will your heavenly Father give the Holy Spirit to those who ask Him?
>
> Luke 11:11–13

You will not lose control.

Some are reluctant to follow the Spirit's prompting to speak in a prayer language for fear that they will lose control of themselves and do something embarrassing. But those who speak in tongues are never described in Scripture as losing control. The purpose of tongues is not to overwhelm or humiliate you, but to bless God, bless others, and edify your own soul. Remember: There is no safer place to be than under the full control of the Spirit of God!

You don't have to join a charismatic church.

If God grants you this gift, continue in your present church. The time you spend in prayer and the joy you experience in worship may increase!

You may well encounter opposition, however, and even ridicule from some. Be patient and loving with them. Don't be defensive.

Allow time for the fruit of this gift to grow. Gain encouragement in a small Bible study group or home prayer fellowship sponsored by a church attended by believers who embrace the gifts of the Spirit.

You may also be told, "Oh, I guess this means you think you're better than we are." This is a tragic misunderstanding not only of the gift of tongues, but also of our relationship to the Spirit's work. Simply reassure people gently but firmly that the gift of tongues has not made you a "better" Christian. Perhaps the best way to respond is by saying, "I don't believe that I am now a *better* Christian than you. I simply believe that I am now on my way to being a better Christian than I was *before* I received this gift."

God forbids us to compare ourselves with others, as if we, because of any gift, were better than they (see 1 Corinthians 4:7). But it is essential that we grow up in our faith and deepen in our devotion to Jesus through the expansion of the Spirit's work in our lives.

You don't have to put your brain on ice.

Praying or singing in tongues does not stop your love for the written Word of God and the deep things of theology. Speaking in tongues does not turn your "gray matter" to mush, nor does it diminish the importance of learning solid doctrine.

I can speak only for myself here, but my love for the Scriptures has grown deeper since receiving this gift. If those who pray and praise in tongues find themselves less inclined to dig deeply into the treasures of the Word, it's not because of the gift of tongues. If there were a connection between tongues-speech and disdain for God's Word, then Paul would have warned us of it. And remember that the author of Romans and other doctrinal treatises said, "I thank God, I speak in tongues more than you all" (1 Corinthians 14:18).

Don't prime the pump.

If you don't speak in tongues, but want to, you don't have to prime the pump by repeatedly saying "banana" backward! Ignore those who might suggest certain words if you are having a hard time getting started. Remember: *The Holy Spirit* gives utterance (see Acts 2:4), not a well-meaning friend. Simply wait upon the Lord and speak the words *He brings to mind*, no matter how incoherent or silly they may sound. They are sweet music to your Father's ear!

Persevere in prayer.

When Paul exhorted us to earnestly desire spiritual gifts, he intended us to ask God for what is our heart's desire. Don't be ashamed of wanting this gift. And don't be discouraged if the answer isn't quick in coming. If the ultimate answer is no, then rejoice in the gifts God has already given you. Use them to His glory and the edification of the Church.

I once received a letter from a highly educated and widely respected lady concerning her experience with tongues. Here is an excerpt:

> For what it's worth, let me quickly relate my own tongues experience. Twenty years ago, in high school, my wild and crazy Pentecostal boyfriend and his Pentecostal cohorts tried every which way to get me—a conservative Baptist girl—to speak in tongues. I wasn't opposed to the idea, but try as they did (prayer,

moaning, speaking in tongues over me . . . everything short of slashing themselves with knives), nothing happened. They came to the conclusion that I was horribly unspiritual and resistant to God's work in my life. I can't say that I was deeply marred by the experience, but it did leave me feeling somewhat wary of the validity of the gift.

In June of this year, the Spirit put on my heart the desire to enter an extended fast. On the fourth day (a really, really difficult day of battling against the physical and mental desire to eat) while I was pouring my heart out to God, foreign and strange words welled up from deep within and came spilling out of my mouth. It was quite a few moments before it dawned on me that I was speaking in tongues. Over the next days and weeks of the fast, I was able to use this gift to battle against severe temptation. I doubt whether I would have had the physical, mental and spiritual strength to complete the fast without it. I felt as though the Spirit of God within was interceding to the Father on my behalf. The gift remains with me. I feel most moved to use it during times of deep intercession or deep praise. "Deep" is the best adjective I can think of—it is kind of hard to describe, but I think you know what I mean.

The interesting thing about this lady's experience is that she was not seeking the gift of tongues but *seeking God* . . . with all her heart, soul, mind, and strength. I'm not suggesting that you must follow her example, nor that you will necessarily receive a new prayer language because you fast and pray—but you might!

Devote yourself to extended periods of praise.

I want to close this section of advice for those who don't speak in tongues (yet) with this simple suggestion: Set aside a time and place where you can be alone with the Lord for a few hours of uninterrupted meditation and worship. Whether you combine this with fasting is up to you. Listen to worshipful music and spend time adoring the beauty of Christ and enjoying Him. Open your heart, open your mouth, and sing forth the love songs He puts in you. What happens next is between you and God.

The Gift of Interpretation of Tongues

The interpretation of tongues may be the most neglected gift in the Body of Christ. It is also one of the more important gifts, because it makes it possible for tongues-speech and its blessings to be used in a gathering of believers. But before looking at what this gift is, let me explain what it is *not*.

This gift of interpreting tongues is *not* the ability to interpret all revelation. Someone with this gift is not necessarily able to interpret dreams, visions, or other revelations. There may well be a *charisma* of interpretation such as Joseph's attributing to God his ability to interpret dreams (see Genesis 41:14–16). Daniel was also enabled to interpret revelatory dreams (see Daniel 2, and 4, and especially 5:14–16). But the gift of interpretation is inextricably tied up with tongues (see 1 Corinthians 12:10).

This gift is *not* the ability to translate a foreign language. All of us have seen translators interpret from one language to another. This is a learned human ability that requires no supernatural anointing of God. Interpretation of tongues, on the other hand, is no less a "manifestation" of the Holy Spirit than the gift of miracles or prophecy (see 1 Corinthians 12:7).

What the Gift of Interpretation Is

The *charisma* of interpreting tongues is the Spirit-empowered ability to hear a public utterance of tongues and translate it into the language of the congregation. It may be a literal, word-for-word translation, equivalent in length to the utterance in tongues. It may be a paraphrase of what was said. But since what is said in tongues is often parabolic or symbolic, the

103

interpreter would explain what was said and unpack its significance, not unlike what an art critic does when "interpreting" a painting and explaining its intent or mood. This would be a broad summary.

I see no reason to think the Holy Spirit couldn't enable someone to interpret a tongues utterance anywhere along this spectrum. Thus, someone might speak in tongues at great length, while the interpretation is brief. It is entirely possible that one interpreter might provide a long, virtually word-for-word translation, while another provides a summarization of its content.

In any case, the movement is always from obscurity and unintelligibility to clarity and intelligibility through the interpretation, so that everyone in the church can say "Amen" to what was said (see 1 Corinthians 14:16). Then the entire Body is edified.

The Content of Interpretation

Earlier, we noted that tongues can be any form of prayer, or perhaps worship, as well as thanksgiving (see 1 Corinthians 14:2, 16; compare to Acts 2:11; 10:46). Interpretations therefore will also take the form of prayers, praise, and expressions of gratitude to God. In other words, *if the focus of tongues is God-ward, so too will be the interpretation.*

This raises the question, Is there any such thing as a message in tongues directed horizontally to people rather than vertically to God? Some charismatic believers assume that when tongues are interpreted, it's often a prophecy. But others have argued (rightly, I believe) that what we ought to hear is worship of God. It is not unlike our experience when we read or meditate on the psalms. We are blessed, encouraged, and instructed upon hearing David and other psalmists praise the Lord. If this is correct, and what is spoken in tongues is not prayerful adoration, thanksgiving, or God-focused celebration, we should be slow to conclude that this was a Spirit-revealed interpretation.

If the interpretation of tongues is nothing more than prophecy, why not just have prophetic words and not bother with the tongues? I agree that interpreted tongues may function like prophecy because they edify and encourage other believers (see 1 Corinthians 14:5). But that is not to say interpreted tongues are identical with prophecy. The latter would be true only if one assumes (and then proves) that tongues-speech is always revelatory.

If what I've said is correct, then many so-called messages in tongues directed to people in the form of instruction, rebuke, or exhortation have not been properly interpreted.

Conclusion

I wonder if the opposition to tongues and its interpretation comes less from careful exegesis of the New Testament, and more from fearful reaction to emotional dynamics. But surely God can be trusted with our emotions as well as our minds! Many affirm God's sovereign control over everything *except* their feelings. One thing I've learned through my spiritual gifts is that God can be trusted to direct and oversee our *experience* of His power, as well as our theological affirmation of it. He can be trusted with our fears as we are willing to risk giving Him full control.

TEN

Letting Your Gift Find You

I f you've come to this chapter having read the previous nine, congratulations! You show interest in spiritual gifts and the role they play in your life. You also demonstrate commitment to the authority of Scripture. Many Christians don't believe this issue is important enough for them to read another book. Often with a pained look, they ask, "Are spiritual gifts really that important?" I'll answer that question by asking a few from what Paul says in Ephesians 4.

Do you think it's important for Christians to get along with each other? Do you value Christian unity? Is oneness and mutual love and a common mind crucial for the life of the Church? Paul said that if we hope to experience this "unity of the faith" (Ephesians 4:13), we must have spiritual gifts (see verses 1–13) functioning in the way God designed them.

Do you believe it's important for Christians to be spiritually equipped to do the work by which the Church is built up (see Ephesians 4:12)? If so, spiritual gifts are essential.

Is knowing Jesus a vital part of the Christian life? That seems like a silly question, but few realize that God "gave gifts to people" (Ephesians 4:8), such as prophecy and teaching and the like, "until we all attain to . . . the knowledge of the Son of God" (verse 13). God has graciously given spiritual gifts to help us deepen and expand our knowledge and enjoyment of "the unfathomable riches of Christ" (Ephesians 3:8).

Most believers long for maturity, theological integrity, and growth. But few realize that these things are all tied to the proper exercise of spiritual gifts in the life of the Church (see Ephesians 4:13–16).

Simply put, there is little hope that the chasm I referred to in chapter 1—the large gap between what Christians say they *know* and the way they *live*—will ever be bridged if we continue to neglect spiritual gifts or relegate the Holy Spirit to a secondary status in the Body of Christ. So, if you have reached this point in the book, I say again, congratulations!

So, What's My Gift?

The answer to our final question of "What's my gift?" is *not* found in a spiritual gifts inventory! Scripture would have us take a far more practical approach. Let me give you some examples.

The next time you're in church or in a small group, pause and ask: "Is anyone physically hurting or suffering from chronic pain?" If so, take your hands out of your pockets, lay them on your brother or sister, and pray for God's healing power.

Is anyone you know distraught or discouraged? Are some finding life too frustrating to bear? If so, take them out for a cup of coffee and listen to their story. Don't theologize about their predicament; they need someone to care. Listen to them. Love them. Pray with them. Invite God's Spirit to show you both what you need to know.

Is anyone struggling financially? Give the person your last $50 and trust God to supply your need.

Do you know people who are confused about some verse of Scripture? Perhaps you're just as befuddled! Pull out a concordance, a study Bible, perhaps a commentary. Study these together. Then put your heads (and hearts) together and invite the Spirit to shed light on your thinking.

Is anyone struggling with sin? Offer to pray for the person. But before you do, sit quietly together and ask the Lord to guide your thoughts and speak words of wisdom. If you sense something, or a thought comes to mind, share it. It might open the door to the individual's heart and bring freedom from bondage.

Does the person you just prayed for report hearing voices in his or her head? Does this person struggle with paralyzing shame, accusing thoughts, and self-contempt? If so, speak the Word of God over him or her with authority. In the name of Christ, command any demonic spirits to leave and never to return. Pray for this person to be filled afresh with the Holy Spirit.

Do you know anyone overwhelmed by the clutter in the garage or that ever-increasing mountain of dirty laundry? Offer to spend Saturday with the person, picking up, washing, drying, folding, and putting away clothes.

What am I getting at? Simply this: If we spend *less time* searching to identify our spiritual gift(s) and *more time* praying and giving and helping and teaching and serving those around us, we increase our chances to walk headlong into our gifting. God will more likely meet us with His gifts as we obey what we already know than while we are taking a spiritual gifts test!

Act First and Ask Later!

So, look for a need and meet it. Find a hurt and heal it. Be alert to the cry for help and answer it. Listen for the voice of God and speak it. Look for what's missing and supply it.

When you do these things, the power of God—the energizing, enabling, charismatic activity of the Holy Spirit—will equip you to minister hope and encouragement to those in need. So, if you're still wondering what your gift(s) might be, *act first and ask later!*

NOTES

Chapter 3 Words of Wisdom and Knowledge

1. Charles Spurgeon, *C. H. Spurgeon Autobiography: Vol. 2, The Full Harvest, 1860–1892* (Banner of Truth Trust, 1973), 60.
2. Spurgeon, *The Full Harvest*, 60.

Chapter 6 Prophecy and Distinguishing of Spirits

1. Charles Spurgeon, *The Autobiography of Charles H. Spurgeon*, vol. 2 (Curts & Jennings, 1899), 226–227.
2. Spurgeon, *Autobiography*, 226–227

Chapter 8 What Is the Gift of Tongues?

1. Jack Hayford, *The Beauty of Spiritual Language* (Word, 1992), 102–106.

SAM STORMS (PhD, University of Texas at Dallas) is the former senior pastor at Bridgeway Church in Oklahoma City, Oklahoma. He is the founder of Enjoying God Ministries, is a past president of the Evangelical Theological Society, and currently sits on the council for The Gospel Coalition. He is the author of numerous books, including *The Language of Heaven*, *Practicing the Power*, *Understanding Spiritual Gifts*, and *The Beginner's Guide to Spiritual Gifts*.

Connect with Sam:

SamStorms.org
Facebook @CSamuelStorms
Twitter @Samuel_Storms